C000227243

Liturgy on the Edge

Pastoral and Attractional Worship

Edited by Samuel Wells

with Richard Carter, Andrew Earis,
Caroline Essex, Jonathan Evens,
Katherine Hedderly, Alison Lyon,
Alastair McKay, Fiona MacMillan
and Will Morris

CANTERBURY
PRESS
Norwich

© The Contributors 2018

First published in 2018 by the Canterbury Press Norwich
Editorial office
3rd Floor, Invicta House
108–114 Golden Lane
London EC1Y 0TG, UK
www.canterburypress.co.uk

Canterbury Press is an imprint of Hymns Ancient & Modern Ltd
(a registered charity)

Hymns Ancient & Modern® is a registered trademark of
Hymns Ancient & Modern Ltd
13A Hellesdon Park Road, Norwich,
Norfolk NR6 5DR, UK

British Library Cataloguing in Publication data

A catalogue record for this book is available
from the British Library

978 1 78622 039 4

Printed and bound in Great Britain by
CPI Group (UK) Ltd, Croydon

To all who make and have made
St Martin-in-the-Fields
an experiment in hope
and a living mystery

Contents

About the Contributors

Richard Carter is Associate Vicar for Mission at St Martin-in-the-Fields, which includes ministry with homeless and vulnerable people and those who are refugees. Before becoming a priest he trained and worked as an English and drama teacher and director. He was Chaplain of the Melanesian Brotherhood in the South Pacific and a member of the community. His book *In Search of the Lost* (Norwich: Canterbury Press 2006) tells the story of seven of his community who died working for peace and the way drama, liturgy and the Christian witness of the community helped to bring healing.

Andrew Earis is Director of Music at St Martin-in-the-Fields. He is a graduate of the Royal College of Music and Imperial College, London, and holds a PhD from the University of Manchester. In addition to his duties at St Martin's, he is a regular producer of BBC programmes, including Radio 4's *Sunday Worship* and Radio 3's *Choral Evensong*.

Caroline Essex has been a lay member of the St Martin's community since 2000. She has taken on a variety of roles, many centred on developing liturgy. After completing a PhD in the history of medicine, she has worked at universities in London and the Midlands, specializing in pastoral care and improving the educational experience of students.

Jonathan Evens is Associate Vicar for Partnerships at St Martin-in-the-Fields. He has a civil service background in employment services and has initiated social enterprise and art organizations.

His work at St Martin's includes developing HeartEdge, a growing ecumenical network of churches and other organizations in the UK and beyond. He is the author of *Despair and Hope in the City* (with Philip Evens, Oxford: Alistair Shornach, 1990) and *The Secret Chord* (with Peter Banks, lulu.com, 2012).

Katherine Hedderly is Associate Vicar for Ministry at St Martin-in-the-Fields. She is a spiritual director and a vocations adviser. Before ordination she was Head of Development for a film and television production company, having trained as a producer at the National Film and Television School.

Alison Lyon has served at St Martin's in many roles alongside a rich mix of clergy teams, across three incumbencies. As well as training to be a death doula, Ali works with individuals and groups as a communications consultant, facilitator and occasional textile artist.

Alastair McKay is a half-time priest at St Martin's. He is also self-employed as an adult educator, facilitator and coach. He works extensively with clergy and church groups, supporting people as they learn, grow and are reconciled with one another. He's the author of *Growing Bridgebuilders: Changing How We Handle Conflict* (Coventry: CPAS and Bridge Builders Ministries, 2015).

Fiona MacMillan is chair of the Disability Advisory Group at St Martin's and a trustee of Inclusive Church. After ten years managing innovative health projects, Fiona studied at the School for Social Entrepreneurs, becoming one of its first fellows. She has been ill since 1997 and combines these experiences in her writing and work on disability, lived experience and questions of social justice.

Will Morris is an assistant priest at St Martin-in-the-Fields, as well as an international tax policy specialist. In addition to the ministry of healing, Will focuses on the connections between faith and the workplace, and is the author of *Where is God at Work?* (Oxford: Monarch, 2015) and *Love thy Colleague* (Oxford: Monarch, 2017).

Samuel Wells is Vicar of St Martin-in-the-Fields and Visiting Professor of Christian Ethics at Kings College, London. He is author of 30 books including studies of how worship forms character, a guide to intercessory prayer and a book of 150 Eucharistic Prayers. He is a member of the Liturgical Commission of the Church of England.

Preface

Liturgy is a team game. This book includes extensive contributions from Richard Carter, and has been enriched by material from Andrew Earis, Caroline Essex, Jonathan Evens, Katherine Hedderly, Alison Lyon, Alastair McKay, Fiona MacMillan and Will Morris. But behind those whose words appear in this book are a host of angels whose song makes St Martin's a living mystery.

Those who have prepared printed liturgies have included Cathy Martin and Elinor Newman, Helena Tarrant and the late Angela Anderson; among the music team have been Tom Williams, Sarah Maxted, Jeremy Cole and Richard Moore; among our singers are the Choir of St Martin-in-the-Fields, St Martin's Voices, the Choral Scholars of St Martin-in-the-Fields, the Occasional Singers and the Children's Voices of St Martin-in-the-Fields; among the verging team have been Jacqui Hance, Tony Cox, Anna Yew, Matthew Horton, Anna Sikorska, Tom Marks, Gary Cain, Lee Fitzgerald, Danniella Downs, Dan Kaszeta and the late Ralph Smith; the clergy and licensed ministers have included Colin Midlane, Sally Muggeridge, Paul Lau, David Jackson and Jeff Claxton; our pastoral assistants have been Catherine Duce, John Falcone, Helen Harris, Andrew Bennison, Georgina Elsey and Georgie Illingworth; our indefatigable stewards have been led by Kristine Wellington and Adam Clark; our ministry has been enriched by our intercessors, servers, lesson-readers and those who offer prayer, anointing and the laying-on of hands, together with our flower-arrangers and bell-ringers.

Of those behind the scenes the churchwardens including Rod Beadles, Gail Elkington, Adrian Harris and Chris Braganza and the PCC set the agenda, backed up by our action groups, sub-committees, task groups, fellowship groups, hospitality team and lay chaplains. Our commercial enterprise led by Allyson Hargreaves models and enables the good practice to which we aspire, and our estates and security team led by Ryan Tyler ensures the building issues are always handled with dignity. Our marketing, events, concerts, retail and catering teams support our liturgical ministry in many ways and our development efforts led by Katy Shaw have enriched our worship immensely. We never forget that our good reputation is in large part earned for us by the work of The Connection at St Martin-in-the-Fields led by Pam Orchard and St Martin's Charity led by Tim Bissett, and partner organizations including our Chinese Congregation, St Stephen Walbrook and the Academy of St Martin in the Fields.

This book is a celebration of that communion of saints, a reaffirmation of our shared mission, and an invitation to new partners to join the dance.

Introduction

Liturgy

Jesus tells the tempter in the wilderness that we are to worship and serve God alone. The Westminster Shorter Catechism opens with the assertion that our chief end is to glorify and enjoy God for ever. Augustine, in book 19 of *The City of God*, maintains that there can be no true justice without right worship. Thus liturgy is the heart of faithfulness, the source of human identity and the foundation of justice.

Liturgy is not a synonym for stiff, hidebound, traditional, reactionary, precious, repetitive, wooden performance carried out by prickly, fussy, obsessive people going through the motions without spirit or truth. It is, historically, from classical Greek times, the *leitourgia*, a public event or gesture carried out to enhance the common good. It is, practically, in Christian usage, the sequence principally of actions and secondarily of words that embody and portray the way the church gathered as a congregation together relates to the God of Jesus Christ and is transformed by the Holy Spirit. These can be formal, written, planned and widely understood, or informal, spontaneous, improvised and dynamic. Most often they are a portfolio of learned and remembered gestures, words and songs that are sufficiently embedded in the individual and collective memory that they provide an infrastructure within which the changing, emerging and seasonal elements of the occasion can flourish and grow.

The secret of leading liturgy is to be so well prepared in spoken, written and sung word and thoughtful action, so immersed in the underlying agenda in prayer and understanding, and so closely connected to the other leaders in relationship and mutual respect, that one can set out in a spirit of relaxed awareness and openness to surprise and the unexpected. The kind of liturgy explored in this book requires more than one person to be bearing this kind of responsibility, concern, immersion and joy. It is a team game, and time spent preparing is less a diminution of spontaneity than an establishment of trust and understanding between the most visible participants; the purpose of which is to maximize the potential of the occasion for embodying and portraying Christian faith and ensure that if the unexpected happens it will enhance the sense of truth and glory rather than destroy it. At the same time liturgy is a shared enterprise on the part of the whole congregation, not a performance carried out on the congregation's behalf.

This book is intended to stimulate liturgical renewal in the wider Church – especially in the spirit of turning challenges into opportunities and seeing 'problems' as gifts God gives us to draw us closer into the mystery of our calling. It is designed as the beginning of a conversation, not the last word. It is offered not as a 'look at me' exercise in claiming one congregation has got it right, nor as a series of templates than can be lifted off the page so that others may bypass the vital process of preparation, immersion and relationship-building; instead it is intended as a humble gift to the wider Church from a community that has, for a hundred years, been a focus of people's hopes and projections, comfort and expectation, within and beyond the Church, in sunshine and in rain, in times of aspiration and in recognition of failure. It comes from practitioners and participants, clergy and lay, who seek to be formed by the three statements in the opening paragraph above, and together see worship as part not only of their ministry to become a community formed by worship but as part of their mission to walk with the troubled, the challenged, the afflicted and the rejected and find God together.

On the edge

The vision statement of St Martin-in-the-Fields is 'At the heart. On the edge'.

One night after I'd taken the evening service a woman stopped me as she was leaving and pointed up at our east window. She said, 'Was it bombed in the War? Is that why it's a bit funny?' I tried as courteously and respectfully as I could to say, actually, the artist intended it that way, and as a community we believe the way the oval nestles in but nonetheless challenges the recti-linear lattice tells us a lot more about how God's grace humbles yet restores our nature than a tidy bunch of identical squares might do.

The truth is, life isn't tidy, predictable and neat. Our attempt at St Martin's to form a community of beauty, truth and goodness in the midst of London's most famous square is never going to be about precision or perfection, and we can't blame the Luftwaffe for the fact that we have a shape that takes some getting used to. We're a complex organization because we've grown organically like a garden rather than being constructed mechanically like a building. We've stayed close to the people that need us and value us, and so we've adapted to a shape that works for them. Legally we're several different organizations, the congregation and the company, the charity, the homeless centre, the Trust, the Chinese community centre, and so on. But everyone thinks of us as one.

The notion of a vision statement has become part of corporate jargon. In general it refers to who and what you really are, and where you believe you're going. When we prepared our vision at St Martin's we bore in mind that it needed to be specific – we weren't looking for noble yet generic sentiments about com-munity and justice and love. We wanted our words not to speak of detached attitudes and righteous stances, but of engaged dialogue and active encounter. We also recognized that, while St Martin's is a Christian church, we include in our life many staff, colleagues, partners and visitors who don't express their convictions theologically, so we needed to articulate our vision in ways the whole community could also embrace. We sought succinctly to refer to the things that everyone associates with

St Martin's, like geographical location, architecture, homelessness, music, broadcasting and food. And we hoped to preserve what our east window represents, that our vision isn't slick and smooth, but rough, ready and real.

What we came up with was, 'At the heart. On the edge.' It's worth stating what this vision means and what it says about what and who we are at St Martin's and where we're going.

Let's start with *At the heart*. This is saying something most obviously about geography and culture, but more subtly about faith and life. St Martin's is, without question, at the heart of London. And, for all our identification with the outcast, it's at the heart of the establishment: it was built by a king, sits half a mile from 10 Downing Street, three-quarters of a mile from Parliament, and a mile from Buckingham Palace. Members of the Cabinet and the Royal Family visit almost every year, and countless famous people come at some stage to celebrate, to honour or to mourn.

But more importantly 'At the heart' refers implicitly to life, the universe and everything. For Christians, the heart of it all is God's decision never to be except to be with us in Christ. That triggers creation, as a place for God to be with us, incarnation, the moment Christ becomes flesh among us, and heaven, the time and space in which God is with us for ever. As a church, St Martin's exists to celebrate, enjoy and embody God being with us – the heart of it all. We're not about a narcissistic notion that we are the heart – we rest on the conviction that God is the heart and we want to be with God.

But in addition to indicating something central in relation to geography, culture and faith, the word 'heart' refers to feeling, humanity, passion, emotion. This means the arts, the creativity and joy that move us beyond ourselves, beyond rational thought, to a plane of hope and longing and desire and glory. It means companionship, from a meal maybe shared in the cafe or a gift for a friend perhaps bought in the shop. At the heart means not standing on the sidelines, telling the government what to do or waiting for the market to swing back to prosperity, but getting in the thick of the action, where honest mistakes are made but genuine good comes about, where new partners are found and social ideas take shape. But it also means genuine care. Not long after I came to this parish a national figure told me his mum, who lives 500 miles from London, sends an annual donation every year to St Martin-in-the-Fields. When he asked his mum why, she said, 'St Martin's cares about what matters.' That's what it means to be at the heart. It means practising and being known for compassion, understanding, love. Not walking away from people when life or the church or health or those close to them have let them down.

And that brings us to the second half of our vision, *On the edge*. In just the same way, this has both obvious and subtle connotations. Most evidently, St Martin's is located on the edge of Trafalgar Square, looking over the splendour of the National Gallery, the honour of Nelson's column and the majesty of the embassies, but also the commotion of tourist and trader and traveller and the pageant of protest and performance. But more generally, the word 'edge' speaks of the conviction at St Martin's that God's heart is on the edge of human society, with those who have been excluded or rejected or ignored. God looked on the Hebrews in slavery, looked on Israel in exile, looked on Christ on the cross, and walks with the oppressed today. St Martin's isn't about bringing those on the imagined 'edge' into the exalted 'middle'; it's about saying we want to be where God is, and God's on the edge, so we want to be there too. A former archbishop said:

> If you ever lose your sense of the intensity and urgency of faith, go and hang out with those who still have it – and the chances are they're among those the world regards as the least, the last and the lost.

That's why we're on the edge: because we want to discover that intensity and urgency for ourselves.

Being 'edgy' is often associated with speaking out on behalf of the downtrodden. We don't do a lot of that at St Martin's, for one reason only: we want to walk alongside the downtrodden so that they can find the courage, the voice and the opportunity to speak for themselves. We're not about swapping persecution for paternalism. But being on the edge does mean facing the cost of being, at times, on the edge of the Church. Some of the issues we care deeply about are not areas of consensus in the Church. We aim to practise what we believe is a true gospel where we receive all the gifts God is giving us, especially the ones that the Church has long despised or patronized. That may sometimes make us unpopular. Being on the edge doesn't have to mean being relentlessly opinionated or impulsively impatient: we're in the persuading business, not the railroading business.

But the 'edge' doesn't just refer to issues of exclusion and disadvantage and injustice. St Martin's seeks to be on the leading edge, perhaps the cutting edge in a number of ways. We have a truly outstanding music programme, of voluntary and professional singers, free and commercial concerts, liturgical and performance events. It's getting better all the time. We're looking to embrace ecological concerns in everything we do, and we're seeking a similar rigour and scrutiny and renewal around questions of disability. We have a creative pattern of art commissions and exhibitions that inspire and challenge and stimulate debate. Most extensively, we have a commercial enterprise that's integrated into the life of our church community, and rather than simply being a source of funds is at the forefront of what we're trying to achieve in London's civil economy. As we're trying to promote and share these commitments more broadly, we're developing a sense of how St Martin's isn't just about central London, but about an ethos that is national and in some respects beyond; and we're beginning to develop the appropriately named HeartEdge, a growing ecumenical network for churches and other organisations in the UK and beyond, to make these connections.

I want to take you back to our east window, and the woman who asked if it was a bit funny because of a bomb blast during the war. Maybe it was a better question than it first appeared. St Martin's is a bit funny. It's made up of people who're a bit funny. We've been knocked out of shape by the wonder of God, or the challenges of life, or both. We want to make something beautiful, true and good together. And that leads us to be both at the heart and on the edge. We're a funny shape for a reason – a reason that we hope glorifies God in heaven and embraces those who struggle on earth. Long may it be so.

Liturgy on the edge

This book comes in five chapters, each with its own emphasis. We begin in the first chapter with ways in which we seek to make worship attractional – that is, something that will draw people in through curiosity, hope or broad sympathy. We would love it if people who had never or seldom been churchgoers flocked to our Sunday 10 a.m. Eucharist and embraced all its peculiarities from their very first encounter; but in practice our central act of worship proves very attractive to people who already have some or great familiarity with conventional Church of England liturgy, and find with us a better or more conducive version of what they already know. So we must find other ways for people to discover, explore, gain confidence in and make their own the glories and joys and consolations of Christian worship – and this first chapter outlines the more successful ways in which we have done this.

In the second chapter we explore a series of occasions that have become a distinctive and integral part of our life at St Martin's – what might be termed sharp-end pastoral services. Here we consider a service for families of the missing, a commemoration of those who have died homeless, a service to support those affected by suicide, and other such occasions. These can be immensely significant events for individuals involved. People speak of attending church for the first time in decades. They are painful, poignant and rewarding in equal measure.

Then we consider the more conventional high days of the liturgical year, as seen in pastoral and attractional perspective. Over time we have taken one occasion after another and tried to deepen its texture and seek to engage a wider range of energy and involvement to make it very special for one constituency of those we seek to reach and serve. These are events that many parish churches mark but we offer here a perspective from our own context, with all its opportunities and challenges.

The fourth chapter considers what worship means when it is not simply a bunch of people gathered at one time for a limited period in one place, but when through various kinds of media, established and emerging, a much larger audience or congregation can be found, served and energized in faith. This is an area of growth for us and potential for the wider Church, and is very much a work in progress.

Finally we offer some more general reflections on what makes good worship, how it can be led well, and what questions are the right ones to ask in addressing both friend and stranger, the outsider who somehow belongs and the insider who somehow never does, the stickler for accuracy and the one alienated by precision.

In all these things we seek the glory of God, the companionship of the body of Christ and the wisdom of the Holy Spirit by triggering and engaging conversations, discernment and shared endeavour.

I

On the Edge of Faith:
Outreach Services

Introduction

We can talk about three broad kinds of conventional evangelism: (1) where the church wants to share something that the culture more generally doesn't think it wants or needs, but the church seeks to offer it in an attractive manner anyway; (2) where the church has something that a particular group knows it wants or needs but is not used to finding in the conventional patterns, practices and programmes of the church; (3) where the church observes something people clearly want or need and identifies ways to make that thing available but gently and respectfully seeks to offer a great deal more besides. The examples in this chapter fall into the second and third categories.

In the second category we find Start:Stop, which perceives that many people living pressured lives and working in intense environments long for a moment of peace, beauty and reflection. Such people invariably only have a few minutes to set aside, so Start:Stop seeks to offer them something deep and help-ful – something that some find in a podcast listened to on bus or tube, but is so much more significant when experienced live and tangibly. In similar vein we find Sacred Space, which serves those who have a longer period of reflective time once or twice a month, but who want to be given the opportunity to rest in their own contemplation rather than have their prayer structured by conventional liturgical expectations. Likewise here we explore the ministry of healing, conceived as an outreach event appeal-ing to people who really want help and prayer and identify with the words of Romans 8.26: 'Likewise the Spirit helps us in our weakness; for we do not know how to pray as we ought, but that very Spirit intercedes with sighs too deep for words.' Such people often don't want the baggage of church that comes with such prayer, so here we suggest a service that gives them what they know they need.

In the third category we present Great Sacred Music, a hugely successful programme running since 2013, which starts with people's enjoyment of popular classical music but gives them reasons for the joy they find there – thus achieving as much music as a concert but as much theological reflection as a crafted sermon, yet all in a playful and unthreatening spirit. And there is an account of our midweek informal evening Eucharist, which attracts those who are drawn to a sacramental life but want to participate directly in liturgy and feel less like spectators.

Great Sacred Music

Samuel Wells

I lived for seven years in North Carolina, a part of the USA comparatively well served for public broadcasting. North Carolina has a classical station, not so different from the UK's Classic FM, and on a Sunday, this being the American South, a good deal of airtime reflects the listeners' devotional, largely Christian, interests. As I would step out of the shower on a Sunday morning I would hear a trailer for the 8–10 a.m. programme. It would begin, ingenuously, 'Did you know that a great deal of the classical music that we enjoy has *religious* origins ...?' – as if it had happened upon a remarkable, profound and little-known truth. I never took the trailer seriously. But I never forgot it.

I became vicar of St Martin-in-the-Fields in 2012. Besides engaging with homelessness and destitution, what St Martin's is most famous for is classical music. St Martin's, besides being the busiest choral and orchestral concert venue in the country, is the only major classical music home that makes a commercial profit, rather than relying on grant support. It successfully offers popular revenue-generating concerts alongside more specialist aspirational events. When I joined St Martin's, two things about this drew my attention. One was that all the best-attended concerts were franchised to external promoters: this meant the principal creative live interface between the public and St Martin's was one in which St Martin's congregation, clergy and staff were communicating little or nothing about their own convictions and vision of the world. The concert programme was seen largely, though not wholly, as a form of income generation; no time was being spent nurturing and highlighting our own professional performers – leaving aside the Academy of St Martin in the Fields, an entirely separate but cordially related organization. The other concern was that there was no cross-fertilization between the public-facing concert programme and the congregation-facing liturgical programme. They were run by different people and happened at different times.

Thus in 2013 we combined the concert and liturgical music departments and sought to strengthen both the liturgical and the performance programmes by integrating them. What St Martin's was trying to do was to identify its classical music more closely with its core identity as an agent of renewal in church, world and Kingdom. Given it was famous for classical music, it wanted to offer clearer messages through that fame that spoke of the mission of the whole organization.

The intention has been to retain the balance between worship and performance, professional and voluntary, aspirational and popular, Christian and people of all traditions, entertainment and challenge, pastoral and prophetic. The first result of this was the idea of creating a hybrid event that took the intensity and spoken content of a worship service and blended it with the accessibility and popular appeal of a classical concert. And this was the moment when I recalled that unforgettable trailer from the North Carolina classical music radio station. And so Great Sacred Music was born.

What we have noticed is that many concert-goers see classical music as a significant aspect of their spiritual quest, and/or eagerly wish to discover more about the origin of much classical music in its theological themes and commitments. Thus we have begun to explore ways in which clergy and musicians can present events that provide both musical delight and enriching commentary on the intent and texture of anthems and hymns. These 'crossover' events, which are both concerts and worship services, and at the same time neither of the above, are developing a large and enthusiastic following. One visitor, on departing from Great Sacred Music, and seeing two or three hundred people gathered, said, referring to the internationally known and hugely influential introduction to the faith run by the charismatic West London Anglican church, Holy Trinity Brompton, 'This is your Alpha course.'

Since 2013 Great Sacred Music has taken place at St Martin-in-the-Fields every Thursday between 1 and 1.35 p.m., usually led by me and performed by the St Martin's Voices conducted by Andrew Earis. It follows a regular pattern: it begins with an anthem; then comes a two-minute introduction followed by a hymn; then a commentary followed by two anthems, and another commentary followed by one or two anthems; then a short introduction to the second hymn; finally, there are advertisements to other parts of the church's programme and a short concluding word followed by a final anthem. In between I offer theological, historical and anecdotal commentary on the music, its origins, references and significance. We work hard to ensure it's not an act of worship in any conventional sense: there are no prayers, the hymns are sung seated, God is spoken about but not spoken to, there are no vestments or processions, there is no especial air of reverence. But it still feels different to a concert – not just because there are four or five interruptions to the music, each with three or four minutes of spoken words, but because those words are designed to highlight the dimensions of the notes and lyrics that have existential significance; some people report having an experience of worship, others sense they are involved in an educational programme, others again regard it as just a more engaging form of concert. One regular attender, noting the humour, the critical engagement with faith, and the playful storytelling, said, 'You have introduced me to a more generous form of Christianity.' What's happening is that churchgoers who

4

want to discover the real significance of the music they know mingle with music-lovers who are intrigued by the theological approach that takes their diverse standpoints of faith, other faith or no faith seriously.

The tendency in the classical music world is either to scorn Classic FM as 'Radio 3 lite' or slyly to admire it for making classical music mainstream and profitable. Our approach is not only to see the commercial potential of Classic FM and what it represents, but to see it as indicating a deeper search for meaning, understanding and depth, which St Martin's is well placed to feed and reward. The secret is not to look for a particular outcome, but to ensure every gathering is stylish, professional, light-hearted, probing, surprising, informative and fun. There are usually salacious details about the composers' real lives, a provocative observation about why a hymn, though popular, is problematic, and a pause to dwell on a sublime turn of word or tune and what makes it so special.

Why are people, who in many cases know very little about composition or theology, nonetheless so often moved by classical music that, in the words of that Carolinian trailer, 'has religious origins'? The answer, we have come to believe, is that they are deeply searching for meaning and truth, and, through disillusionment or habit, have in many cases lost the will or desire to seek a fulfilment of that quest in institutionally shaped conventional religion – yet may be drawn to such depths by music that opens doors, asks questions and addresses longings. All Great Sacred Music does is to take that quest seriously and point out the ways that composers of words and tunes were asking similar questions and addressing comparable yearnings.

As Great Sacred Music has become popular, we have sought to adapt it to different settings. One that has proved successful is an evening concert series we call 'Great Sacred Choral Classics'. This is an hour-long format without hymns that takes a theme or composer and offers around 38 minutes of music and 22 minutes of speech. That amount of speech gives ample opportunity to develop a theme in some depth. Thus, for Mozart's Requiem, familiar choral pieces were interspersed with five-minute addresses on Death, Heaven, Hell and Purgatory. For Haydn's

Creation a similar format allowed for addresses on Haydn, creation, science and ecology. For 'Jesu, Joy of Man's Desiring' there were addresses on Bach, Jesus, joy and desire.

Another successful spin-off we call 'Making My Heart Sing'. This is a blend of the BBC Radio 4 classics *Desert Island Discs* and *With Great Pleasure*. A celebrity is invited to choose around eight favourite choral pieces and then is interviewed in a conversation that explores their life and convictions about faith while linking together the eight choral pieces, each of which is performed live. Again it lasts one hour.

Example outline – International Women's Day

Anthem 1: O virtus Sapientiae (Hildegard von Bingen)

Welcome and brief remarks about:

- Hildegard of Bingen
- International Women's Day
- three kinds of feminism found within the Church and theological thinking
- Bernadette Farrell, author of the first hymn

(choir standing, everyone else seated)
Hymn 1: 'O God you search me and you know me'

Brief remarks *(largely about the connection between Anglo-Catholicism and the women's suffrage movement, as featured in anthem 3)*

Anthem 2: Jesus Christ the Apple Tree (Elisabeth Poston)

Anthem 3: Sanctus from Mass in D (Ethel Smyth)

Brief remarks *(about Edith Cavell's faith and life)*

Anthem 4: Standing as I do before God (Cecilia McDowell)

Brief remarks *(about Irish Anglo-Catholic hymn-writer and social activist Cecil Frances Alexander)*

Hymn 2: 'All things bright and beautiful'

Closing remarks and announcements *(concerning Amy Grant, known as the Queen of Christian Pop)*

Anthem 5: Thy Word (Amy Grant)

(35 minutes in total)

Start:Stop

Jonathan Evens

St Stephen Walbrook, a partner church of St Martin-in-the-Fields, is located, midway between Bank and Cannon Street stations, on Walbrook, one of the busiest streets in the City of London. Between 7.30 and 9.30 a.m. a human river of souls flows up and down the street, all, until recently, passing St Stephen by, as the church was not open until later in the day.

The Parish of St Stephen Walbrook is populated by the insurance and financial industries, with other small businesses including restaurants, solicitors, banks and retail outlets. The parishioners are therefore the employees of these companies, rather than local residents. The key to mission in the parish is relationship with the major local employers, but, with changing work patterns and increased time pressures, the traditional midpoint in the working day when employees might frequent the City's many churches has been increasingly squeezed. The average lunchbreak in the City is 22 minutes.

As the mission challenges and opportunities at St Stephen were discussed, it became clear that this early morning flow of workers should become a key focus for the church. But what might engage busy people spilling out of crowded trains, grappling with the pressures of the upcoming day? And how could we encourage them to divert from their walk to work in order to come to church?

Our thought processes were as follows:

- Because of the pressures working people are under, whatever we offered had to be brief. That seemed to rule out all of the traditional Anglican services as, however much one pared them down, they were likely to be longer than the amount of time that busy people could spare. This gave us a clean slate from which to work in designing our liturgy. We decided that whatever we offered should last no longer than ten minutes.
- Although brief, what was offered had to give sufficient value to warrant people altering their usual schedule. We thought that content needed to relevant, so had to be work-related.
- Because working life is pressured, we thought the time should be (and should be publicized as being) contemplative and reflective, as this could assist the well-being of workers in stressful circumstances.

Thus emerged the following initial parameters: ten minutes in length; work-related content; contemplative in nature; and non-traditional format. As a result, we decided to trial the use of a brief Bible reading, a short work-related meditation, space for silent reflection, and a responsive prayer, ending with a blessing. The prayers were to be based on the content of the meditation and the response would specifically use a phrase taken from the meditation, in order to unify the ten-minute session we were spending together. To assist in creating a contemplative atmosphere, we would play instrumental music quietly in the background and dim the lighting.

To enable people to drop in as and when they could and to guarantee that they would have to be there for no more than ten minutes, it was agreed that each ten-minute session would be repeated every 15 minutes from 7.30 to 9.30 a.m. on a Tuesday morning.

We decided to call the session 'Start:Stop', with the strapline 'Start your day by stopping for 10 minutes of quiet reflection', and created a flyer using traffic lights as a visual equivalent of the title, 'Start:Stop'.

To publicize Start:Stop we thought we would have to get our materials directly into the hands of those passing the doors of the church, so we leafletted on the street in the weeks running up to the launch.

We also thought that busy people would need a physical visual reminder of the sessions each day that they were occurring, so we created large signs which could be held up high on the street directing people to the church entrance for '10 minutes of quiet reflection'. For one of us physically to be on the street would, we thought, witness to a ministry of presence – and so it proved. The signs, as well as providing a visual prompt at the moment people are making a choice as to whether or not to come in, also led to other snatched conversations, and are a talking point to which people refer when we meet them in other contexts.

The result has been that between 30 and 60 people regularly attend Start:Stop. These are people who were not previously attending St Stephen Walbrook. They tell us that ten minutes is manageable for them at that time of day and that, because the content of the meditation is directly relevant to their work, the session sets them up for the rest of their day. Some will stop after the session to share a pastoral need or a request for prayer, while others have begun coming to services and activities at St Stephen Walbrook more generally.

Start:Stop is an example of contextualized ministry that works with (while sometimes also challenging) the actual and real experience of working people. As a result, connections are made between faith and work, and the church is seen to be supporting the well-being of working people through its pattern of worship and pastoral care.

Example outline – Show us how our humanity can be made 'salty'

Welcome and brief outline of the session

Bible readings: Matthew 5.13 and Mark 9.49–50

Brief meditation based on the readings:

- About the use of salt in preservation and flavouring.
- 'Every gift you have been given … these have been given to you so that you can work with God to unlock the full potential of his world' (G. Kelly, *Humanifesto*, Spring Harvest, 2001).
- Brief summary of the five different relationships that the Christian can have with culture as proposed by H. Richard Niebuhr in *Christ and Culture*: opposition, agreement, Christ above culture, tension and reformation.
- Let us ask God to show us how our humanity can be made 'salty', both in its role on the earth and in our workplaces.

Silent reflection

Three responsive biddings using the response:
Show us how our humanity can be made 'salty'
in our role on the earth and in our workplaces.

Blessing: Being granted a vision of our world as God's love would have it, unlocking the full potential of this world, using every gift we have been given, using our gifts for the common good. May all those blessings of God almighty, the Father, the Son, and the Holy Spirit, be among you and remain with you always. **Amen.**

Closing announcements: reflection concluded, so feel free to leave; invited to stay longer should you wish; time of next reflection; thank you for coming.

(10 minutes in total)

Sacred Space

Richard Carter

Many of our acts of worship are very word-focused. So much so, that when we think of creating a new liturgy the usual place to start is with what words, readings, hymns or sermon will be included. It becomes an order of worship printed on a service sheet. Yet we have discovered at St Martin's that among many there is a growing thirst for greater contemplation and silence: a need to move beyond words and the printed page into a deeper space – the place of encounter. We are 'called home', as St Augustine put it, 'from the noise that is around us to the joys that are silent. Why do we rush about ... looking for God who is here at home with us, if all we want is to be with him?'[1] In the contemplative tradition there are techniques to help the individual find this inner space: the use of prayer words or phrases, or simple repeated prayers like the rosary or Jesus prayer.[2] And because deep contemplation includes our whole bodies and our senses there are physical ways of helping us to still the body which involve the way we sit, our posture, our breathing. There are also other aids to finding this still place, like candles, music or the use of a visual focus like a cross, icon or painting. What all these techniques help us to do is leave behind the distractions and anxieties of the day and find a place to be present with Christ.

Many people today are talking about the importance and benefit of 'mindfulness' and meditation – the way it can improve the individual's sense of well-being and quality of life. Of course techniques of mindfulness and meditation have a very rich spiritual tradition within the Christian faith. I would like to use the word 'presence'. How can we create a time and place where we are truly present to ourselves, to God, to one another and to the world in which we live? And how can God become more present to us? It can often seem that the church is a place that simply

---

1 St Augustine, *On the Trinity* VIII, 7.11.

2 Martin Laird, *Into the Silent Land: The Practice of Contemplation*, London: Darton Longman & Todd, 2006), pp. 34ff.

makes us busier and bombards us with even more words and activities and interactions. Many of us may have resolved to keep a time of quiet prayer only to find a few weeks later that this time has been eaten away by other commitments. When we have tried to pray on our own we sometimes find these quiet times are anything but quiet. Instead of a still place, we enter into what can at times feel like a jumble or chaos of memories, thoughts, hopes, desires and fears. It is in this place of unknowing that what Martin Laird, in his very helpful book *Into the Silent Land*, calls 'the commentary' begins: we find our minds not only flooded with thoughts and feelings but also a commentary on them. Such a commentary, far from moving the prayer from head to heart, makes our minds even busier: 'Who have I forgotten to contact? What shall I do? How can I cope with so and so? What's the point of this?' The silence we needed and sought is very different from this troubling introspection.

It is clear that our silent, contemplative time needs discipline and a structure that can help free us from such commentary. One of the communities that has done much to provide that access and structure into such a contemplative tradition is the Taizé Community in France. What Taizé has done so successfully is to open up the monastic tradition so that all can participate in that experience of the sacred – including beginners. Many young people, including myself many years ago, discovered a deeply resonant form of prayer at Taizé that made us thirsty for the beauty of God's presence among us and awakened a longing in our hearts to recapture that experience in our own prayer life when we returned home. In many ways Taizé taught me and many others to pray in a deeper, more meditative way and to enter into silence as a way of discovering God's presence. But how does this experience translate? With the Taizé brothers in our midst, the flickering candles and the ever-repeating beauty of the chants, it feels to many they have discovered the prayer of the heart. But it's not so easy on their own or in their home churches when the liturgy seems more formulaic and so less spacious and there is so little silence. What are the elements that members of the Taizé Community use to help liturgy move from our heads to the soul of our being?

- They create welcoming space – a place of silence and of sanctuary that is open day and night for people to enter into. It is no accident that it is the warmest place in the community. There is a very palpable sense that this place of prayer is the very centre of community life.
- They provide a sense of openness through the absence of fixed furniture. The carpeting and use of prayer stools creates a simplicity, an equality, but also helps us with posture, so essential to meditative prayer: by modelling our own posture on that of the monks – using a stool or prayer cushion to keep our backs straight – we learn to pray attentively with the crown of our heads in line with the base of our spines. This allows for a deep sense of reverence but also for a posture that can breathe in the prayer deep within us: a prayer not of the head only but that can come from the very centre of our diaphragm.
- The icons, with their simplicity and beauty, become visual points of focus, windows or doorways into the divine.
- The use of candlelight and natural light increases the ambiance of the sacred.
- It is the music of course for which Taizé has become rightly famous – simple beautiful tunes that can be taken up by all; simple words from Scripture repeated again and again and again so they cease to be something we are reading but rather something we are listening to with the ear of our hearts.
- The liturgy moves into an extended period of silence. Silence is at the very centre of the liturgy. The central focus of the liturgy is therefore listening rather than telling. I remember so clearly the founder of Taizé, Brother Roger, teaching: 'Let us listen to God: God's wisdom is so much better than my words.'
- And there in the midst of us are the Brothers themselves, called to live this life of prayer and contemplation, whose reason for being there, and for holding the whole day in prayer – morning, afternoon and evening – is God.

So how can St Martin-in-the-Fields in its own way create a sacred space in the centre of London? We are not trying to re-create

Taizé but to learn from the practice of the contemplative tradition. Around us in Trafalgar Square is all the noise, traffic, energy, creativity and intensity of this capital city. How can we enter into a prayer that soaks up the needs of the city but finds a way of transfiguring those hopes and fears through the stillness of God's presence? We have tried to find that sacred place through a tradition enriched by many different communities and individuals. This is what we have done at St Martin-in-the-Fields, which I offer as one adaptable pattern that could allow contemplative prayer to flourish in your own church.

1   We found a time when people were searching for a quiet and more contemplative space: a time on Sunday when for a moment the centre of London stills just a little. We chose 7.00 p.m., a time where 'the shadows lengthen and the busy world is hushed'.

2   Our Evensong finishes by 6 p.m., so there is time to create the sacred space into which people are drawn – without rush or anxiety. The Taizé cross or another icon is placed on the chancel steps. A number of candles are lit at the foot of the cross and on the ledges behind the altar. A Taizé CD is played quietly as people gather.

3   Cushions, prayer stools and, behind them, benches are placed around the cross or icon for those who will gather.

4   We have fixed pews in our church. We have learnt repeatedly that it's initially hard to get people to abandon the safety of the pews to come in and sit on the floor. Especially if they are newcomers, they invariably want to sit far from the front and scattered, rather than together with others who have come. And so our service provides a way for them initially to have this space and then for them to come forward and join others in a way that is non-threatening and inclusive. At the front of the pews we provide baskets of votive candles.

5   We use a small music team – a pianist, a guitar player and a soloist – and sometimes a further instrumentalist – a violin, a flute, an oboe. Sometimes there's just the piano.

6   The service begins simply with a song or chant and then a welcome to all who have chanced to come into this sacred space.

7   One short passage of Scripture is read, followed by a short reflection. We have found it is important that the reflection is not a long sermon but simply a few words that open the passage up, allowing people to enter into the words read, to be fed by the word itself rather than a complex exposition or specific application. We are inviting people to be attentive to the presence of Christ in our midst, revealed in his word but also revealed in this group of people gathered in his name.

8   Then we come to the time of gathering, in which those scattered around the church are invited to light a candle and place it on the step, at the foot of the cross. The lighted candle is a sign of Christ present in each of the lives gathered. We often say to people as they receive the candle, 'You are the light of Christ.' As they place the candle they make their own silent prayer. Before they come forward we invite them, instead of returning to their places, to stay around the cross or icon, on the cushions, prayer stools, benches or front pews. It seems that the lighting of a candle is an action that allows everyone to respond naturally to this gathering. The one leading the service also sits or kneels among those gathered.

9   In this gathered space now the singing of chants begins, often sung in different languages. Often the words of the chant are read first, and those who are gathered are gently invited to put down any pieces of paper they are holding so that the simple repeated words can become their own prayer: the prayer of our hearts. The repetition deepens the prayer, allows it time to filter through the layers of our lives and consciousness. It allows the prayer to become as natural as the air we breathe.

10 These chants lead into an extended period of silence. One often fears the silence, fears that here in the very centre of London it cannot hold. The noise from outside, the sirens, the shouts from the street, the events in the square can intrude. But in the silence of the church we are invited to let go of all the noise and disturbance, both without and within. It is not an empty silence but one the prayer has led us into – a silence charged or infused with presence. Hold on to that. Hold it even when you feel it is ready to burst. Let go of the

coughings and the restlessness and stay with the silence. It is in this silence that we enter together that place of unknowing where our lives are untangled and we glimpse the height, breadth and depth of God's presence. A presence of which we are part.

11 After the silence there are simple prayers – often no more than a single line or petition, the more spontaneous the better; nothing complex, just an expression of need and a longing for God's healing grace. Each petition is followed by a sung response.

12 This service ends with a final hymn or chant or song, followed by a blessing for all those who have come – a prayer that we may be the bearers of Christ's presence back into the world, holding this sense of God's indwelling within us, a presence beyond words. No one wants to rush away. Many remain kneeling in front of the cross before leaving quietly. Many whisper as they leave, 'That was so beautiful', or, 'That was just what I needed', or simply, 'Thank you'.

I cannot stress enough the importance of a shared space for meditative prayer and silence. We often wonder why we don't do this alone and indeed we can. But there is something very powerful and supportive in being with others as together we enter into a period of silent contemplation. It is the silent prayer of those around us that deepens, enriches and enfolds our own.

An example of a simple order of service – The sound of sheer silence

Introit: 'Te lucis ante terminum' (To thee before the close of day) (soloist)

Welcome and introduction

Hymn: 'Be still for the presence of the Lord'

Reading: 1 Kings 19.4–12

Reflection

Nunc Dimittis (Geoffrey Burgon) (soloist)

As we gather lighting candles and placing them in front of the icon or cross we sing

'My peace I give you, my peace I leave you' (Taizé)

Having gathered sitting on the floor, benches and kneelers around the cross we then sing

'Wait for the Lord' (Taizé)

'The Lord is my light' (Taizé)

'"See I am near" says the Lord' (Taizé)

'Christe Domine Jesu'

Long silence

Short intercessions with sung response

Take, O take me as I am

You are my salvation I trust in you (Taizé)

Final blessing

'This Day' (Bob Chilcot) *(soloist)*

Prayer for Healing and Laying-on of Hands

William Morris

The root of Christian healing lies in the incarnate ministry of Jesus. The Gospels contain numerous stories about illnesses being cured, disabilities being removed, and evil spirits being cast out to restore wholeness – often by Jesus laying his hands on others. While these are miracles, they are not magic tricks done to startle, or even to edify. Jesus makes clear that healing and wholeness come because our sins have been forgiven – a burden has been lifted from us. And he also always makes clear that the healing comes about through the grace of God and is activated by our faith ('your faith has made you well').

Even in his Galilean ministry, Jesus sent the disciples out to heal the sick, to lay on hands and to anoint with oil. And after his death, the apostles continued this ministry of healing to those troubled in body, mind or spirit. Anointing with sacred oil is a tradition often mentioned in the Old Testament as setting people aside for God, as well as bringing succour and comfort through divine grace. The Letter of James specifically calls for the Church to anoint the sick and to pray for them (James 5.14–15). So, while not strictly instituted by Jesus, anointing with oil and the laying on of hands became one of the seven sacraments of the Church.

In the early Church this tradition continued with physical healing being associated with laying on of hands and anointing. But the increasing association of anointing with repentance and penance, as the Church moved into the Middle Ages, meant that anointing was only done when physical healing was highly unlikely and death was near ('extreme unction'). So, while the Church continued to care for the sick as a charitable endeavour, and figures such as St Francis of Assisi continued the tradition of healing, the link between anointing and healing lapsed.

The reinvigoration of healing as a Christian rite really started with the Pentecostal (charismatic) movement of the early twentieth century and the 'rediscovery' of the gifts of the Holy Spirit listed in 1 Corinthians 12.8–11, which included healing. As a result, over the course of the last hundred years both the Roman Catholic Church and many Protestant denominations have returned healing to its place as an important sacrament in the life of both the community and the individual.

The new Anglican liturgy, Common Worship, provides services for both healing of the community as well as for individual healing through the laying on of hands and anointing. At St Martin's we offer both. And while we would not deny the miracles of

Jesus, or the possibility of divine miracles today, we understand (and offer) healing more broadly. Healing is the restoration of wholeness: it may well not be full medical 'cure', or 'going back to the way things were before'. But healing is our caring, loving God giving us the strength and comfort to carry on. And while our understanding of healing fully accepts – and encourages – the role of medical (physical and mental) treatment, we also understand that, as Jesus taught, wholeness may require spiritual healing. So, forgiveness and reconciliation are also an important part of the act of healing.

We have experimented with various types and formats of healing services at St Martin's. Sometimes healing may be required for a community or for a country or for the world, but often the most acute need will arise for individuals in relation to illness, a broken relationship, a work crisis or a similar event. Thus, one of the features of this ministry is that the aim is not necessarily to build a worshipping community or long-term congregation, as such. To turn that around, because this ministry is often most needed at moments of crisis, while it may not be a regular service for any individual (although it *can* be), it should be a regular, sacramental offering of a church available to all individuals on the occasions upon which they need it.

We have incorporated elements of healing in special services (St Luke's Day), separate services (an evening standalone service, or combined with compline) and as a sacramental supplement to other services (after Sunday Parish Communion). All of the varieties of the service we have tried share a common approach (and progression), which can be summed up in three words: silence, touch, words.

- First, silence. We listen to the person amid a deep listening and openness to God. We open ourselves to be a channel of God's healing and peace for this person in whatever way God chooses to use us. We need silence to centre ourselves, to be sure as those administering healing that we are not bringing our own troubles into the encounter. Then, we should be silent so we can listen very carefully to what the person seeking healing is saying.

- Second, touch. Touch creates a human connection, establishes a relationship between the two people. It is both a symbolic and a practical gesture, empowering the person seeking healing to share with and rely on the other.
- Finally, there are words. While this must be preceded by silence and touch, words are necessary to confirm release from what it is that troubles that person, and also to send them back out into the world from which they came. The final words of blessing are generally also accompanied by a final physical act – the anointing with oil.

Here are some reflections on what we have learnt. We must always be aware that for many who come to this service, they are in a very dark, very vulnerable place. Particularly for those who have been sexually or otherwise physically assaulted, 'touch' must be very carefully and sensitively done. Usually a light touch on the head or shoulder will be entirely appropriate, but we should watch and listen very carefully.

It should be made very clear in as many ways as possible (order of service, verbally and physically) that the healer is in a position of total equality with the person seeking healing. The 'healer' is not the bounteous giver, but a fellow traveller with the person seeking healing. (To emphasize this equality I often sit on a bench in the sanctuary with the person seeking healing.)

We are privileged (amazingly, immensely privileged) to stand alongside those seeking God's help and wholeness, but we do it as brothers and sisters, ourselves in need of healing. To that point, before or after others come up for healing, the healing team should themselves seek and receive prayers for healing from other members of the team.

While this is a sacramental act, we do have a mixed team of ordained and lay healers, partly to emphasize that everyone can be this channel of God's healing grace, but also, again, to emphasize equality with those seeking healing.

We need to be aware that there are some things we will not be able to deal with – severe mental illness, for example – and we should always be prepared to counsel seeking medical help while offering spiritual relief. Leading on from this, we should never put ourselves or others at physical risk. It is prudent to work in pairs, rather than doing it singly, and also to have members of the healing team present in the congregation to help with troubled individuals, should that need arise.

Example outline – A Sunday evening healing service

- Before the service there should be music. Taizé or something similar is often helpful to set a mood of calm. Many people come to the service troubled, scared or embarrassed to talk about a need for healing, and this lead-in helps with that. Members of the healing team pray together and hold silence to settle themselves before God.
- To start the service there is a welcome and introduction, which helps not only explain the structure of the service but also sets expectations about what constitutes 'healing'. There are then short prayers, a communally sung Kyrie (Lord have mercy) and a communally said psalm. There is then a Bible reading. Normally we do not have a reflection on the reading, but there could be one at this point.
- A member of the choir then sings a solo. After experimenting, we decided this should not be done during the prayers for healing, as it might distract or overwhelm, but that it did mark a good break between 'word' and 'sacrament'. People are then invited to come forward to the altar rail/into the sanctuary. It is made clear that God's healing is available to people whether or not they come forward.
- Before anyone comes forward, the healing team themselves (in full view) seek prayers for healing from other members of the team. It is helpful to have a team member guide people forward. This enables a space (for privacy) to be kept between those receiving healing and those waiting to receive it.
- The person seeking healing is asked to say their name and what/who the healing is for.
  - The healer may gently touch the person on the head or shoulder/upper arm.

- First, the person seeking healing should say for what they seek healing – but the team member should also sensitively ensure that this is not too extensive (sometimes by inviting them to stay afterwards to talk more).
- Then the person administering healing should pray quietly but audibly for the concerns mentioned. Again, this should not be too lengthy, and it is as well to have some appropriately pastoral phrases ready, as well as responding spontaneously to the concerns presented. Ideally touch may be maintained throughout this time, although circumstances differ.
- Finally, the anointing should take place, with comforting words of dismissal (such as: 'Go in the healing love of God').
- During the prayers for healing, music is quietly played. This offers dignity and privacy; the music should not be intrusive.
- After everyone has returned to their seats, there are prayers of thanksgiving, ending with the Lord's Prayer. There is then a communal song or hymn. The service closes with a final blessing.
- Depending upon time and the size of the team, members of the healing team can make themselves available for more extensive conversations after the service.

Informal Eucharist

Richard Carter

A Eucharist can sometimes feel like a drama performed on our behalf by the designated ministers. A church can be like a theatre with a proscenium arch – most of the action taking place on a stage from which the audience is spatially separated. The members of the congregation become the witnesses, the listeners to prayers offered on their behalf. They are read to and preached to without interaction. In the sacrament they are recipients. The only things that are participatory are the responses to prayers which are prescribed and the hymns with words and a tune that they (mostly) adhere to. For much of the service the congregation are static – they do not move other than to stand up or sit down until they come up to receive Communion. Most of the physical action of the liturgy is done for them.

In the theatre, many directors have experimented with trying to remove the divide between the actor and the audience to create a greater sense of involvement. The aim is to create not so much a spectacle in front of us but an event actually happening to us, in our very midst, in which we all become the actors. As we developed our informal Eucharist at St Martin's we talked about how we could change the shape of our liturgy so that all could participate more fully in the action of this sacrament, while at the same time not losing its reverence. If all who gather are called to be part of the one body then they are the liturgy themselves.

We gathered a group together to experiment with different ways we might do this. We experimented with not using the altar at all but gathering around a small table sitting on the floor. We experimented with movement so that the offertory became a procession around the church in which everyone participated. We experimented with paperless liturgy where there was no prescribed response. At our Parish Away Day we held a silent Eucharist where no words were used at all but all of us were invited to participate in the actions which make up the Eucharist. It was beautiful. From these experiments and thoughts we have created an informal Eucharist which has been used every Wednesday. Our liturgy has been formed and shaped through repetition so that people can feel familiar and comfortable with that shape, and yet we have tried to allow for this liturgy to also maintain a sense of spontaneity and immediacy: the sense that this is not just a repetition of past actions but Christ made present and in our midst now. In all of this we have been careful not to lose the sacredness and beauty of the Eucharist, nor its simplicity or power. Not 'do it yourself' but a Eucharist in which each one of us is called to be intimately involved, just as those first disciples were involved as they shared the Last Supper or met the risen Christ when he broke bread at Emmaus. There is nothing very revolutionary in the form we have arrived at but it does have an immediacy and engagement that has built a small mid-week community who come regularly to this Eucharist each week and then for a simple supper afterwards followed by reflective listening groups sharing their responses to the theme or Gospel they have heard. We have discovered that the most important thing is to keep this Eucharist as simple and natural as possible. We are not aiming at a performance but at something transparent: God's life in our midst and flowing through each one of us. We call this informal Eucharist 'Bread for the World'.

This is the pattern we have developed.

1 All who come are warmly welcomed when they arrive by some of those who come regularly to this service and whom I will refer to as the community. They are not given a service booklet but a single sheet, which includes the hymns or chants and a couple of responses. They are invited, but not forced, to take seats as near the front as possible. In front of the pews are some benches and wooden kneelers, bringing a greater closeness. There is no procession but all those taking part take up their places as part of the congregation around the altar. This includes a group of our choral scholars without choir robes who sit together.
2 The choral scholars begin with an anthem or song that introduces or helps create the ambience or spirit of our theme. During this piece of music two members of the community come forward and simply prepare the altar for the Eucharist – 'preparing a place for Christ'. They light the candles, spread out the corporal (the white linen cloth) and place the pottery chalice, into which they pour wine, and the pottery paten, onto which they place fresh bread.
3 The celebrant welcomes those who have come, inviting them to participate in this Eucharist and later to join us for a simple supper. We want to establish a sense of the generosity and beauty of Christ's invitation which is extended to all.
4 There is a simple participatory confession.
5 One of the community reads the Gospel.
6 The reflection is usually shared and over the weeks has involved a large variety of people from all walks of life, including those from the community, choral scholars, guests

and invited speakers. It has taken various forms, sometimes an interview, sometimes different speakers, sometimes something more participatory, like the use of drama or Godly play. It is important to hear the voices and reflections of some of the youngest or newest members of the community. Also the voices of those seldom asked to speak, like homeless people, or those who may sometimes feel on the edge of more formal gatherings. Obviously these need to be sensitively prepared and it helps to have someone interviewing who is known and can hold and weave this together.

7 After the reflection, members of the community lead the prayers, which they have prepared in advance after reflecting on the theme, and all of us join in a sung chant response to each of the prayers.

8 The celebrant now shares the peace and invites everyone to gather in a circle around the altar – a circle in which all are included. There is a hymn, song or chant as we gather.

9 The Eucharistic Prayer uses different voices. We have tried to make it direct and immediate, allowing for spontaneity so that it can draw on the theme we have shared. The words of consecration and the calling upon the Holy Spirit are said by the celebrant but we have tried to make these words present tense: something that is happening here and now and that unites all those who have gathered.

10 In one circle we say the Lord's Prayer together.

11 The sacrament is shared around the circle, with members of the community offering the bread and wine as the choral scholars sing. Those who do not wish to receive keep their heads bowed.

12 At the end of the service once again all those who have come are invited to continue the Eucharist with a simple shared supper and the chance to share thoughts and reflections with one another in groups.

13 The meal that follows the Eucharist is as simple as possible – usually bread and soup prepared by our cafe. The focus for this is not the food itself, the preparation of which could easily begin to dominate. The food after the Eucharist aims to continue the Eucharist as we talk and meet.

14 After this we divide into 'listening groups', led by regular group leaders who encourage a sense of belonging for all, newcomers and regulars. We have found that between 8 and 12 people in each group works best. There are simple ground rules for these groups which we discuss together. The understanding that we are here to listen to one another, that each person is given space, that these are not competitive groups or groups trying to argue that one individual's point of view is the correct or best informed one: rather we use Scripture as the means of encountering how God is at work in the lives of others. Each session begins by listening to the presence of God in Scripture through a short *lectio divina* on the passage we have used in the Eucharist. We have found it best to go round the group making sure that each person is given space to speak. This sharing ends with prayer.

Example of the full liturgy

Gathering

Music or song as two members of the congregation prepare the altar and light the candles

> We light these lights for the Trinity of love:
> God above us, God beside us, God beneath us:
> God at our centre
> God on the edge
> God with us.

Prayer of invocation

> We prepare a place for you
> Come to us in the difference of every life gathered
> Come to us in song
> Come to us in word
> Come to us in stillness
> Come to us in bread and wine

Come to us in flesh and blood
Reach out across time
Be present in all time.
Come Jesus, be our guest,
Stay with us for day is ending.
With friend, with stranger,
With young and old,
With the lost and found
Be among us tonight,
Our guest, our host,
The one who says all – all are welcome here.

Song or chant

Prayers for forgiveness

Because the world is beautiful
but beauty is easily destroyed,
we need you.
Lord Jesus Christ, son of God, have mercy on us.

Because we are weak and fail,
because we cannot live without love
but often walk in darkness,
we need you.
Lord Jesus Christ, son of God, have mercy on us.

Because we often abandon you
and turn away and walk past
and are afraid
and countless times fall short of your goodness,
but you love us to the end
and win a victory over all hatred,
We need you.
Lord Jesus Christ, son of God, have mercy on us.

Because we have your message to proclaim,
because we have your kingdom to build,
because there are so many in need of your love,

because we have your life to live,
we need you.
Lord Jesus Christ, son of God, have mercy on us.

And Jesus said, 'Your sins are forgiven'.
In the name of the Father who created you and waits to
welcome you home,
in the name of the Son who searches for you,
in the name of the Spirit who brings the healing of
forgiveness
and calls you to do the same,
you have been set free.
Amen.

or

Lord, you look upon us with love, knowing our weaknesses
better than we know them ourselves and knowing how often
we fall short of your glory. Let us confess our failures to keep
your ways of life and truth.
Silence

Lord, we have put ourselves first and failed to love you and
fallen short of the fullness of life that you long for for us.
Lord, have mercy.
Lord, have mercy.

Lord, we have hungered and thirsted for our own comfort
and safety,
and turned away from the injustice done to others.
Christ, have mercy.
Christ, have mercy.

Lord, we have been divided against one another in hatred
and pride, and failed to live as peacemakers and bearers of
your love to our sisters and brothers.
Lord, have mercy.
Lord, have mercy.

May the God of love and power
forgive you and free you from your sins,
heal and strengthen you by his Spirit,
and raise you to new life in Christ our Lord.
Amen.

Word on the Edge – a passage from the New Testament is read

Reflection

Silence

Prayers are offered

Members of the congregation offer the following prayers

A prayer of thanksgiving
Sung response
A prayer of concern
Sung response
A prayer of hope
Sung response

The sharing of the Peace
God of eternal peace,
who offers the gift of peace
and whose children are the peacemakers;
pour your peace into our hearts,
that conflict and anger may cease.
The peace of the Lord be always with you.
And also with you.
Let us offer each other a sign of that peace.

*Song or chant, during which all are invited to gather in a circle
around the altar*

The table
Lord Jesus Christ,
you have invited us to come to this table.
We have come from many places and experiences;

we have come with all our differences;
we have come to the place where journeys meet.
You have reached out to all on the edge
and called us into the heart of God.

The Lord be with you.
And also with you.

Reader   On the night that Jesus was betrayed he told us to
prepare a place for him. And then he offered us a sign.
A sign of how he would give himself to us to give us
new life. He had always loved us, and now he showed
us how perfect his love was.

Priest   While his disciples were eating, Jesus took a piece of
bread in his hands, like this, and he blessed it:
Blessed are you Lord God of all creation;
through your goodness we have this bread to offer,
which earth has given and human hands have made,
it will become for us the bread of life.
And then he said to them:
This is my body broken for you, do this in
remembrance of me.

Silence

Reader   And then Jesus took a cup of wine, like this, and gave
you thanks:
Blessed are you Lord God of all creation, through your
goodness we have this wine to offer, fruit of the vine
and work of human hands,
it will become for us the cup of salvation.
And then he said to them:
Drink this all of you,
this is my blood of the new covenant which is shed for
you and for many for the forgiveness of sins.
Do this in remembrance of me.

Silence

Reader His disciples did not understand these words; how
could they understand? But later they would see
Christ's body broken, his love poured out – his death
for us so that we might share his risen life.
The life he gave then, he shares with us now.

Lord Jesus Christ,
as we do in this place what you did once and for all,
breathe your Holy Spirit upon us
and upon this bread and wine
that they may be heaven's food,
renewing, transforming, sustaining and making us whole;
so that we may be your body on earth,
loving and caring for your creation,
where all are welcome
and the poorest are fed.
Bless the earth,
heal the sick,
let the oppressed go free,
and fill each one of us with your love from on high.
Gather your people from the ends of the earth
to feast at your table with all your saints.

The Lord's Prayer

Fraction and invitation

Priest Look, Jesus Christ, the Bread of Heaven, is broken for
the life of the world.
The gifts of God for the people of God.
Jesus, Bread of Life
Bread on the Edge
Bread for the world.

*Song or chant as the bread and wine are shared around the
gathered circle of people*

Thanksgiving

God of hope, in bread and wine you have restored us to
relationship with you. Show us how to be a people that live
your reconciling love in the world, so that we may recognize
your presence in those we meet, and our hearts like those first
disciples may burn within us upon the road.
Lord Jesus Christ,
You are the Word for us to speak,
You are the Truth for us to tell;
You are the Light for us to light in the darkness,
You are the Bread of Life for us to share.

Now all of us must go out into the world
And live God's love there.
Look for Jesus in the oppressed and burdened,
Look for Jesus in those who have lost hope,
Look for him among the poor in heart,
Among the merciful
Among the peacemakers
Among the persecuted for the sake of right.
Look for Jesus on the edge.

Song, chant or hymn

The Blessing

Go simply, lightly, gently.
Go with obedience.
Go with love.
And the blessing of Almighty God,
Father, Son and Holy Spirit be with you now and for ever.
Amen.

Song of blessing

2

On the Edge of Life:
Acute Pastoral Services

Introduction

Some of the most profound moments of the liturgical year at St Martin-in-the-Fields come in the services outlined in this chapter. Several times in the New Testament we are reminded that the stone that the builders rejected has become the cornerstone. Usually that is taken as a reference to Jesus, his rejection by his people and his vindication in resurrection and ascension. But in the experience related in this chapter, we have discovered that the stones rejected by the world become the cornerstones of God's Kingdom. Sometimes that rejection is accidental, sometimes deliberate; either way, God is renewing the Church by populating the Kingdom with those who, like Israel in Babylon, discover that God is sometimes closer to us in exile than in the comforts of the Promised Land.

All of these services began with an approach from external agencies, who saw in the spirit and ethos of St Martin's a suitable community and location to host the fragile yet beautiful message they were seeking to convey. In every case we long for each service to be the last such occasion that is necessary – and yet, in most cases, a year later there still seems at least as much to pray about and ponder together. In every case the key themes are lament and solidarity. These services have become almost a trademark of what St Martin's at its best is all about: finding beauty and truth in the wilderness and on the margins.

Those Affected by Homicide

Richard Carter

For more than 20 years each December St Martin-in-the-Fields has held a commemoration service for those bereaved by homicide. Sadly the need is very great. In the year ending March 2015 there were 516 homicides recorded by the Home Office. Over 35 per cent of these were caused by a cutting or stabbing with a knife or sharp instrument. While these statistics are grim enough, the very nature of homicide means that it does not involve just the tragic loss of life of these 516 individuals; it also involves the grief, trauma and lasting suffering that is caused to the family and friends of the one murdered, as well as all those connected with the perpetrator. In other words, this is an event that has an impact upon the whole of somebody's life and community. Not only do the families and friends of the bereaved suffer the terrible grief of losing a loved one so suddenly and violently, they also have to grapple with the knowledge that someone has done this to their loved one, and all the anger and resentment, bitterness, hatred, pain and violation that brings. In addition, they will often have to go through very lengthy police investigation processes, which can be incredibly traumatizing and by their very nature make the victims' loved ones often feel that their evidence is not being listened to or acted upon quickly enough or, still worse, treated with suspicion. Another of the factors involved is that many people find homicide almost impossible to talk about or relate to after the event. When the homicide has taken place in a public place to someone young there may be an initial outpouring of grief, which has often found expression in the bringing of flowers to the scene of the crime, or the lighting of candles, or a vigil or public gathering and of course the funeral. At this time everyone expresses their horror and shock about what has happened and there may be public attention and sympathy. The problem is that for those bereaved the grief does not end there but begins there. The initial numbness and shock gives way to the realization that nothing is going to bring the loved one back, and the realization that this life has been wilfully cut short by someone. Families and friends bereaved by homicide often find themselves feeling increasingly isolated and cut off from their community. The events of the homicide are too painful and extreme to share, and yet the grief and the trauma are continually in the minds of the bereaved. Trauma like this often leads to clinical depression, and the breakdown of relationships. In a family everyone may have a different way of responding, leading to division, further stress and feelings of survivor's guilt.

The Rt Hon. Kenneth Clarke, in his Foreword to the *Review into the Needs of Families Bereaved by Homicide*, wrote: 'Of all the consequences suffered as a result of crime, the anguish experienced in those cases where a relative is killed stands alone.' Every single person in a survey said that the experience had affected their health; 25 per cent never worked again; nearly half the families experienced divorce or separation from a spouse. Post-traumatic stress disorder is a real possibility, even decades later. Nothing is ever the same again. Everyone who has suffered such a bereavement says that it changes your life unalterably for ever. On the other side, the community often feels powerless to engage with the bereaved after the initial period of grief is over. There is a fear that you will say the wrong thing or stir up the memory. Consequently there is a kind of silent agony that develops after a homicide, where the bereaved feel alienated and that no one really understands this most overwhelming and terrifying loss.

The Annual Commemoration Service for those Bereaved by Homicide provides a public expression for this outpouring of grief, remembrance and love. It is also a witness to others of the horror that violence causes and that no one should ever have to suffer. The service provides the opportunity for people who have been through the horror and pain of this loss to gather to support, share and simply be with one another. Many of those who come have been coming back year after year. Some of them lost a loved one through homicide longer than 20 years ago, but this act of remembering has become an acknowledgement that, though parted, the loved one has never been forgotten.

I have been helping to prepare these services for the last ten years and there are things that we have learnt together along the way that I would like to share as they may be helpful for those who in tragic circumstances find themselves called upon to support those bereaved in this way. These points are very simple and seemingly obvious ones but they are offered in humility simply as things to consider.

1 Being with. We often back off because we do not know what to say or how to help. One of the things that we can do as church is to simply be there for the person. This may mean simply being present – being with the bereaved, listening, not judging or offering platitudes or solutions, but being alongside the person in their trauma and grief.

2 Being constant. There will be a lot of people who will come and go – police, neighbours, wider community, media, victim support officers, solicitors, doctors, counsellors – and enter into the life of the bereaved. The church can be the community that was there before the tragedy and will continue to be there for the person after the tragedy.

3 Being a safe space. The church can provide a sanctuary to which people come. It is also one of the few places of inter-generational community where people of all ages can come together in mutual support. It is a place to which the whole family of the bereaved can come.

4 The church provides the language of both life and death. Though many people may question how God could allow this suffering to happen, the church is one of the few places that reflects on the meaning of life – and the meaning of death. The church is also one of the few places that provides a place of stillness and quiet for reflection, prayer and remembrance.

5 The church must be initially most of all the place of listening. There is a real temptation to try and find the answer to a person's grief, to short-cut it, rather than to be the place where that grief can be expressed. The person who ministers will often want to try and lessen the anger and the pain by talking of healing and perhaps even the importance of things like letting go and forgiveness. This healing takes time and

it is really important to allow the bereaved themselves the time to discover that healing or that forgiveness, or not, as the case may be. The bereaved will often feel it is a violation of the memory of the loved one for anyone to talk about forgiveness.

6   A memorial service aims to help find a way to express the grief and allow the bereaved to feel and experience the solidarity of others. For those who feel they have been the victims of a violence that has not only taken their loved one away but also injured them too, this commemoration allows the opportunity to express this loss to others who have been through a similar experience themselves.

7   There are many groups, charities, or foundations set up to offer advice and support, usually by those who have lost loved ones. We try to work closely with these groups and those bereaved so that the service is their own. In the 20 years since this memorial began, this service has been co-ordinated by Justice for Victims, KnifeCrimes.Org, and most recently Support after Murder or Manslaughter (SAMM).

8   The service is put together by a team, which includes input from these organizations, with SAMM most recently becoming the lead organizer.

9   The service consists of readings, testimony, music and reflection, and leads to a simple symbolic action where each of those bereaved is invited to come forward to light a candle for the family member, friend or loved one murdered.

10 Each year different people are chosen to give the reflections. Those who come are the ones who know the reality of the loss and the process of grief. As far as possible it is good that they be involved in leading both the reflections and the service, but they need sensitive support for them to be able to do this. The most helpful testimony comes from those who have experienced this kind of loss first hand.

11 There are music contributions, from our choir but also by singers who themselves have experienced the loss of someone they have known through violence.

12 A memorial book is kept of those who have died and each year the new names are added.

13 At St Martin's this service takes place in December and so carols are often used. This may seem an anomaly, but this works well in that carols are both comforting and also tell the story of love incarnated in our world – a child who will also face, even as an infant, the horror of violence and later a violent and horrifying death, a child who will nevertheless reveal that goodness is stronger than evil and love stronger than hate.

14 After the candles have been lit, the families themselves have introduced a tradition where rose petals fall softly from the balconies of the church upon those who have come. For me it has always expressed something of the nature of love and healing which is beyond words and falls upon us with the softness and grace we were not expecting. We are surprised by a love that is both beyond us and within us.

15 The refreshments and reception that follow are also important, allowing families and friends to meet with others who have been through similarly traumatic events. There is much compassion and real understanding from those who have known a similar grief and faced the trauma that a murder leaves in its wake. There is a deep sense of connectedness and empathy, and many comment that the service was very moving and beautiful and each year they will come back again. For they will never forget.

An example of the introduction to the service and service outline

On behalf of St Martin-in-the-Fields I would like to welcome you all to our Church for this Annual Memorial Service especially for the families and friends of those bereaved through homicide.

Today more than ever we live in a world blighted by acts of senseless violence and the fear of violence. In the last year in London knife crime is up by 4 per cent and there were over 4,000 knife crimes in London alone and guns were fired 302 times in this city. Last year there were 573 homicides in the UK, a rise of 11 per cent. And, as we all know, violence is not just about events which take place in gangs out on the street but within people's own homes, often perpetrated by those known to the victim. Neither too can any of us escape the images of the suffering of our world at this present time, wherever it may be, in Syria, Iraq or Yemen. Violence, murder and homicide are difficult words to deal with. It does not just affect one person, it affects the whole family, the loved ones, the friends, the whole community. It is the wound we all carry with us, which can never be forgotten.

But what is also true is that again and again we have experienced the importance of this act of remembering, remembering not just privately but together with those who understand, really understand because they have been through a similar suffering themselves. And there is a shared hope – the knowledge that those we loved and hold in our hearts live on with us, and we will never ever forget them or walk alone. It is as though the tragedy can also release in us the knowledge of where we stand and the values we believe in. From the place of tragedy, we see life in a different way: a new truthfulness, compassion and longing for justice can be born. I know all of you here today have been changed by tragedy, and in your hearts have said 'never again' – this should never happen to others. I know many of you have used your lives to try and make this world a better, more just and safer place for others, and to support others who have been through tragedy and pain. You are doing that today. Today as we come to remember those who have died as victims of violence we also celebrate the birth of Jesus Christ. He too was murdered in the most terrible way imaginable, and the mother who loved him and bore him would witness his death. But we celebrate his life because it is his love and goodness which lives on and not the misguided evil of those who killed him.

I say we have come to celebrate because what Christmas celebrates is that love cannot be put to death, it lives on. We too come to celebrate the love we have for those from whom we are parted – the times we shared, the unique people they were, their gifts, talents, strengths and failures, their dreams that made them who they were. Today we come to give thanks for each of their lives and to celebrate that love is eternal and nothing in heaven or on earth can ever separate us from that love.

Welcome

Congregational hymn: 'O come all ye faithful'

Poem

Choir: 'The Lord's my shepherd' (Howard Goodall)

Testimony

Choir: 'One hand, one heart' (Leonard Bernstein)

Poem or reading

Soloist: 'O holy night' *(sung by one of those who has been bereaved)*

Reading: 1 Corinthians 13

Address

The lighting of the candles. *All those present are invited to light a candle in memory of the person who has died. These can either be placed on votive candle stands or other suitable place at the front.*

During the lighting of the candles the choir sing 'Silent night' and 'Make me a channel of your peace'

Minute's silence and throwing of petals

Choir: 'Like a candle flame' (Graham Kendrick)

During which the Communal Candle is lit and the Memorial Book brought forward

Words of remembrance

Prayers of hope

Congregational hymn

Words from the chair of the charity or group who have organized the service.

Soloist: 'You'll never walk alone'

Blessing

Choir: 'The Lord bless you and keep you' (John Rutter)

Those Affected by Suicide

Samuel Wells

In 2014 St Martin's was approached by the Alliance of Suicide Prevention Charities to explore holding a service to stand in solidarity with those affected by suicide. It quickly became apparent that this meant three broad kinds of people. The first and most visible were parents of those who had, mostly in their late teens and early twenties, and often after a long struggle with mental health challenges, taken their own life. The second were other family members – spouses, siblings, children. What marked the parents out from other relatives seemed to be that the parents were more likely to have founded charities or in some other way become active in supporting other families or advocating for measures to make suicide less prevalent. The third were those who had themselves attempted suicide, often more than once, and had reached a place where their life was no longer in the same degree of crisis and were willing to speak about what they had been through and offer support to those whose stories had worked out differently.

In beginning the conversation I was aware that this was a group of people who might well have misgivings about the Church. Some might feel that churches were full of self-righteous, 'together' people who might have little sympathy or tolerance for those whose lives were so evidently troubled or had been so manifestly scarred. Others might simply not share Christian convictions about forgiveness and eternal life and be uncomfortable around those who did. But a more significant concern might be that suicide has often been condemned among the churches. Roman Catholics who had committed suicide were until recent decades denied a church burial, and the Catholic Church still officially regards suicide as a mortal sin. In these circumstances the concern of families in approaching a church is understandable. What made St Martin's a suitable venue was not simply the dignity, size and accessibility of the building but the congregation's reputation for humane and sensitive understandings of a whole range of pastoral issues.

The instigator of the service, David Mosse, names the issues succinctly:

> Love, it seems to me, is why suicide is so difficult and so utterly painful. Love is that human condition which means that we none of us own ourselves, we have and are shared selves. Suicide is an act within this world of relatedness – often in response to unbearable emotional pain rather than the desire to abandon us – but which tears apart and contradicts what is essential to our very being.

And the damage is long-lasting. As Simon Critchley puts it:

> When someone dies by suicide, those bound by love often experience a shadow of the pain and anxiety that preceded the death they grieve; and the guilt. Guilt because, in the search to understand why, we are so connected that we make ourselves the first accused. As we continue our search for answers, suicide saddens the past [at the same time] as it abolishes the future.'

The planning meetings for the first service were thoughtful and probing, and the service was considered such a success that it has become an annual occasion. For some, such grief is an intensely personal matter, and the circumstances are sometimes so distressing that it can be hard to share the story with a stranger.

Others find that a single appearance at such a service is cathartic: after one service a person said to me, 'It's the first time I've been in a church for 30 years, since that day.' One thing that became apparent was that the experience of the person who has considered, perhaps attempted, but nonetheless emerged from the shadow of suicide is very different from the experience of those bereaved by suicide. The first is a story from despair into hope; the second is a story of grief that may not be helped by premature words of superficial consolation.

The service has remained very similar in structure each year. Like most liturgy, it traces a journey: in this case one in three parts. The first part takes seriously and attempts to meet head on the genuine dismay and horror of losing a loved one to suicide. It speaks the language of lament, testimony and pain. The second part addresses the more ambivalent experience of attempting suicide and surviving to tell the tale. It articulates what is going through the mind of a person in crisis, but also how those thoughts can be modified and even healed. The third part tentatively hints at solace, in wisdom if not in joy, in solidarity if not in closure, in goodness if not in transformation. In the words of David Mosse, the first part concerns 'the loss of self, of connection, of meaning, or of hope that precedes suicide; and the unbearable loss faced by those bereaved'. The second part he describes as 'the experience of fear and isolation, especially that inner isolation of those in despair; and the guilt after loss that blocks the path to self-care'. And the third he regards as 'finding the strength to endure, to heal and find purpose, and to help ourselves out of solitude, especially through reaching out to one another'.

To accompany each stage there is a threshold action, accompanied by suitable words. For the first threshold, 'Lost', a rock – heavy, sharp, uncompromising – is laid down, and these words spoken: 'In these rocks we see brokenness, harshness and pain. We see love cut off, a statue destroyed, a future shattered.' For the second threshold, 'The Valley', a candle is lit – fragile, small, yet burning – and these words are spoken: 'In this candle flame we see fragility, possibility – the shadow of what is half-known, half-understood, still mourned.' For the third threshold, a rose is laid down – beautiful, prickly, tender – and these words are said: 'In this rose we see gentle beauty, still with thorns that pierce, yet deep tenderness, hopefulness, deeper truth.'

It goes without saying that silence and music – choral, instrumental, solo contemporary – are at least as significant as anything spoken or enacted. To hire outstanding singers and musicians isn't within everyone's budget, but for the poignancy of an occasion where words cannot ever cover the range of emotions involved, music is vital. While congregational participation in such an environment – which must remain hospitable to people with diverse and often complex feelings about faith – needs to be handled with care; one hymn with a haunting tune seems to be about right.

It's important to offer serious but gentle words of welcome, such as these: 'We've gathered today to talk about something that usually evokes silence – silence of shock, pain, terror and loss. We're gathered to stand in solidarity about something that often keeps people isolated – in despair, grief or guilt. We've gathered to find hope together that we perhaps struggle to find alone.' Besides compelling testimonies and helpful readings, two spoken contributions are given prominence. At the beginning is an address from the key person responsible for bringing the service about, speaking from the heart about losing a son, but also from the head about the nature of suicide and the approaches to its prevention, and setting a reflective and tender tone for all that follows. At the end is a clergy address. More than most sermons, this is about tone of voice more than content, about compassion and understanding rather than proclamation or exegesis. One year I talked about the film *Lion* and how it addressed issues of loss, depression, failure, isolation, identity and narrative. Another year I spoke about silence, touch and words as a response to grief. Another time I explored what it means in the words of Isaiah 43 to be precious, honoured and loved.

Vital to the whole event is the opportunity to gather informally afterwards over coffee. It's a unique pastoral moment: small talk is unnecessary – everyone is there because their lives have been shaped for ever by suicide in some way. Conversations emerge rapidly and honestly. For many it's a cathartic moment. Some have travelled far simply to be present. Others have never been in a space where their tragedy has been addressed with kindness, understanding and beauty.

We call the service Time to Talk because it is, more than anything, an opportunity to overcome isolation. Again, to quote David Mosse, speaking of his lost son:

> Understanding why he, and so many like him – facing incomprehensible pain and despair – felt that to die was the only solution; and making other solutions more thinkable and accessible for those in this desperate state, is the challenge we all face. This is a challenge made so much harder by the stigma and silence that allows suicide as an option to grow in the dark corners of tormented and isolated minds. This perilous silence has to be broken. It really is 'time to talk about it'.

Service outline

Introduction

- Instrumental music: 'Largo' from Oboe Concerto No. 3 in G minor (George Frederic Handel)
- Clergy welcome
- Opening address
- Choral music: O thou that art the light (Gabriel Jackson)
- Lost
- Laying a rock (*action and words*)
- Testimony
- Choral music: *The Lamb* (John Tavener)
- Poem
- Sung solo music: 'Dido's Lament' from *Dido and Aeneas* (Henry Purcell)
- Silent reflection
- Choral music: Agnus Dei from *The Armed Man – A Mass for Peace* (Karl Jenkins)

The Valley

- Lighting a candle *(action and words)*
- Testimony
- Solo contemporary song
- Testimony

Found

- Placing a rose
- Testimony
- Choral and instrumental music: *Gabriel's Oboe* (Ennio Morricone, arr. Craig Stella John)
- Clergy address
- Hymn: 'Be still my soul'
- Choral music: *Cantique de Jean Racine* (Gabriel Fauré)

Those who have Died Homeless

Richard Carter

Each year we hold a service for those who have died homeless in the last year. It includes the names of those in London who have died homeless or vulnerably housed in hostels or temporary accommodation for homeless people. It is a deeply moving service with over 350 present, including many who have known homelessness themselves or who work to bring help and support to homeless people either professionally or as volunteers. For 90 years St Martin-in-the-Fields has been known for its work with homeless people. It is also a church which each year holds the memorial services of many important and well-known people. Side by side with such memorials, this commemoration has a special poignancy and importance. It aims to express the dignity, care and respect that each human being deserves both in life and in death. Last year 160 names were read out. Throughout the

UK the number of people in need and homeless on the streets has dramatically increased since 2008. Sleeping rough can be very detrimental to people's physical and mental health, meaning that the average age of death for someone on the streets is just 47, compared with 80 for the general population. Homelessness can happen to anyone. This service is a recognition of the struggle, pain, loneliness and poverty but also of resilience on our streets, together with the goodness and the presence of Christ in the midst of all that can dehumanize.

Early in the year a group holds the first of four meetings to plan the service. The group includes an artist, Don Pollard, who has himself been homeless, and representatives from St Martin's, Housing Justice and The Connection at St Martin's. The Connection is London's busiest homelessness charity supporting people away from the streets through specialist services, including a day centre, night centre, street outreach, help finding employment, and specialist mental health and addiction support.

Our aim in the service is to involve homeless people themselves and allow for the expression of sorrow, but also thanksgiving for the uniqueness and humanity of all those who have died, especially those who may have died without friends or family to remember them. Many of those on the list are the names of foreign nationals who have died far away from home. But while the service has an advocacy element, that is not its main purpose, which is to commemorate before God and one another these many human lives. The service centres on the reading out of the names of those who have died. This is then followed by a symbolic action in which the whole congregation are involved. One commemoration service was entitled 'In my Father's house there are many rooms'. In front of the altar we built the frame of a house, like a triptych, two metres high and three metres wide. At the beginning of the service the two doors of the triptych were closed. Covered with black felt, there was just the black silhouette of a house. After the reading of the names, the doors of the house were opened, revealing a bright yellow, dancing Matisse-like figure. All who had come to the service were given, as they entered, cards with the name of one person who had died, illustrated with a similar dancing figure. During the symbolic action, each placed their card within the frame of the house, so the house was filled with the names and dancing figures of those who had died. It was a simple action but one in which it was deeply moving to participate.

The doors of the 'house' are opened

Placing cards in the 'house'

The finished triptych

The reading of the names of those who have died

The names are read out in four groups. After each group, one of the names in that group of names is spoken about. It is a brief insight, a window into a life – a character and the way they have impacted upon others: an anecdote, an amusing story, or a struggle they had, or a moment of hope. Sometimes our knowledge of the lives of those who have died is painfully thin. Other lives seem rich and vibrant and chaotic and colourful. Each name a human being with all the hopes and fears of the years they have lived. Those invited to tell these stories are members of different homelessness agencies. Often people who are homeless themselves, or who have been homeless, have volunteered to share a few words or read a poem or prose piece they have written. These memories are followed by a silence kept for all those names. This silence each time is bookended by the ringing of a bell.

The symbolic action

Each year we have chosen a different theme and created a different expression of remembering each name. One year we created a river with fish, another year a vine with many branches, another angels ascending and descending on a ladder that rose high above the altar. One of the most beautiful was when we chose the theme 'Consider the lilies' and each life was remembered with fresh lilies brought up and planted in front of the altar – more than 400 lilies in bloom, filling the church with their fragrance. We want always to create a movement so that those present are involved physically in an act of remembrance rather than simply as witnesses.

Music

We have a music group with guitar and piano and sometimes flute and violin. We want the music to be inviting, rather than austere and formal, so as to draw us into these lives. But sometimes, for instance at the end of the service, we use the organ to unite all our voices. We also use choirs of people who have known homelessness themselves and what the fear and vulnerability of homelessness mean. Both of these choirs, Streetwise Opera and Choir with no Name, are inspiring in their own right. These choirs give people a voice; there is a raw energy, passion and lack of self-consciousness, an expression of heart and soul.

Reflection

A good reflection at a service like this is an expression of all that Christ is, while at the same time avoiding the formulaic language of religion that can alienate and polarize. So, for example, rather than talk about the Trinity we talk about relationship; instead of being redeemed by the cross, we talk about how love and forgiveness can save us. Instead of talking about the homeless, we simply talk about people. Instead of talking about charity, we talk about how whatever we do for the least of our brothers and sisters, we do for Christ.

The place of remembering

This service provides the time, space and structure for the church to become an important place for remembering, healing and affirming. In a sector where there has sometimes been a division between the faith-based and the secular, this service is a real chance for all to come together and find shared values and a deeper unity. The church, through careful preparation and inclusive liturgy, has the unique opportunity and role to restore dignity, affirm human truths, and publically remember the story of people's lives. After the service there is a reception at The Connection to which all are invited. It is an occasion where all mix and interact freely without distinction. I remember a homeless person called Lesley saying to me: 'Why do they call us "homeless people". We don't call them "in-house" people. We are all just "people".' Amen.

Throughout the year

This service has provided a valuable opportunity throughout the year to build further relationships between the church and those who have known homelessness. When one of The Connection's outreach team died it was the church that was able to provide the space for the staff and clients to express their grief and to celebrate his life. We have also been able to provide funerals and vigils for those who have died on the streets, often in tragic circumstances – offering space for people to express their grief and trauma and to celebrate lives that have often been hard and painful. The church can thus become a place of healing and of hope that truly belongs to all of us. In January every year we always keep Homelessness Sunday to remember all those people who are still homeless.

Service outline

Musical introit

Welcome and introduction

Hymn: 'Abide with me'

Reading: Psalm 23

Reading: John 14.1–7

Reading of the first set of names

Prayer of remembrance

Silence

Sung response

Reading of the second set of names

Prayer of remembrance

Silence

Sung response

Reading of the third set of names

Prayer of remembrance

Silence

Sung response

Reading of the final set of names

Prayer of remembrance

Silence

Sung response

Explanation of symbolic action
You are invited to place the card of the dancing figure you have been given as you came into the church within the open doors of the house in front of the altar – the house of many rooms in which all are welcome. As you return from the altar you are invited to take a card with the name of one of those who have died written on it and remember that person during the coming year.

The symbolic action

Songs

Music: 'Heroes' (David Bowie)

Reflection

Music: 'You'll never walk alone' (Rodgers and Hammerstein)

Lord's Prayer and Blessing

Hymn: 'And did those feet in ancient time'

Those who are Missing

Katherine Hedderly

The charity Missing People and the Missing People Bureau of the National Crime Agency approached St Martin's in 2011 about a Christmas carol service to remember those who are missing and their families who long for their loved ones to come home or be found. Many have waited and searched for years, and Christmas is a particularly poignant time with its message of hope of a transformed future but also a time when coming home to be together as a family makes their loss all the more painful. The service aimed at assuring the families that they are not forgotten and was also a way to raise awareness of the charity's 'Home for Christmas' campaign. St Martin's work with those on the margins and care for the vulnerable, including those experiencing homelessness, meant that the church was a good home for this special service. What began as a carol service has, over the last six years, become a community event and a source of hope and action for all involved, with many families coming year after year to share experiences and find support. Some have just recently had a family member go missing and are coming for the first time, others are living with a loss spanning many years. There are good news stories too of those who have been reunited, and where it is possible to share these stories we do. The church is always full for this service (825) and it has led to similar services in other cities around the country: Liverpool, Manchester, York, Edinburgh, Cardiff, Chester. A choir drawn from families of the missing and supporters began at the service three years ago and is now nationally recognized, recently taking part in a television series, which led to one family being reunited and to leads in another case.

From the outset we worked on making this a service of presence, addressing the limbo that the families were living with a real incarnational engagement with loss and hope, not a jolly sticking plaster of Christmas cheer. We involved members of the families throughout, along with their supporters, representatives of the police working in this field and high-profile charity patrons. From the beginning we included testimonies from those who had family members missing, input from the police, along with actors and celebrities coming together to contribute to the service. Kate McCann, a patron, has been a regular contributor, as have other families in the public eye.

Before and after the service the charity family support group host a social event for family members in the large rooms of the vicarage, which allows families to meet up, share news and support one another, with 60 regulars. St Martin's has therefore become an important place of welcome for families themselves to come home to each Christmas. There's a Christmas tree, people know their others' names and recognize them, and important conversations take place in this social setting. For some this is the only time they will meet up during the year and it is an important pastoral opportunity for the clergy leading on the service. One woman who had come for the first time said it had taken her 40 years to begin to talk about her sister who went missing as a teenager, and coming to the service for the first time was a way to begin to speak about her loss. An event for the charity's spon-sors, led by their development team, takes place at the same time in another part of the site, supported by our events and cafe staff.

The service includes elements of a traditional carol service, choir pieces from our own choral scholars and well-known carols, but it also involves at least one family member speaking about their experience, the police representative and director of the charity giving reflections, as well as the families' choir's input in recent years. The symbolic action of family members lighting candles from the Advent candle and sharing that light around the full church is always a high point of the service. The action is empowering for the families and important as together we hold that liminal moment between loss and hope. The ones who carry the greatest loss are also the ones who share the light, the symbol of hope and life.

Working with the police has developed over the years as they have been encouraged to share stories rather than statistics and facts, one of the most moving contributions being the story from a missing person's point of view, as we heard what it was like for him when he was found through an encounter with the police and supported as he made the difficult journey of reconnecting with his family.

One year Kate McCann, mother of Madeleine McCann, and Coral Jones, mother of April Jones, read a poem together that one of them had written. It was a moment of strength and dignity. Together they were able to hold the fragility of their suffering and remember their children. Both mothers of young daughters, one abducted and not yet found, the other whose daughter was tragically murdered in her own village. For us that evening they were like Mary who was full of joy at the birth of the Christ child but whose soul was pierced at his death on the cross. Their strength was a transforming moment that gave us the hope of resurrection, the light of new life.

The Missing People Choir has been a special development. It began when Peter Boxell, whose only son Lee Boxell went missing from Cheam in Surrey in September 1988 aged 15, wrote a song in his memory and sang it at the service. He said about the choir:

> There isn't a minute when your heart is free from pain and heartache. Having the support of each other makes us stronger, singing together makes us 'super strong'. We all have to live in hope. If there's no hope, what do we have to live for, there would be nothing. Our common goal is to find our missing loved ones and bring them home where they belong.

Choir member Sarah Godwin, whose son Quentin has been missing since May 1992, and who is also a trustee of the charity, said: 'It's just so energizing, warming, safe, moving beyond words. We can each feel our own love and sadness and pain, but we are there for each other and somehow it becomes joyful too.'

This is a service that is not afraid to go to the depths and to shine a light into the experience of living with loss day by day. It is countercultural to the upbeat contemporary Christmas going on all around the families. It is real, and when we get it right it connects to a deep joy that promises that God is really Emmanuel, with us, even in this experience of life, that the light does shine in the darkness.

Service outline: Missing People Carol Service – Together in hope that they'll come home for Christmas

Introduction:

> Christmas is a special time of year where families celebrate together. But for the many people we support, it is a heart-breaking time full of anguish and worry. The only gift they hope for is that their loved ones will return safe and well. This evening we will hear from families who have experienced the joy of being reunited, we remember those who are lost and we gather together in hope that those who are missing will come home for Christmas.

Music before the service (Royal Mail Choir)

Congregational carol

Clergy welcome and opening prayer

Welcome on behalf of the charity by the patron

Poem *(written by family member of someone who is missing)*

St Martin's Choral Scholars: Candlelight carol (John Rutter)

A story of hope *(by the mother of someone whose son returned home)*

Missing People Choir: 'All I want for Christmas is you'

Reading from Scripture

Carol *(with solo by choral scholars)*

Poem *(read by family member)*

On hope: a contribution from a representative of the National Crime Agency or local police

Congregational carol

Reading from Scripture

Words from a family member about the experience of waiting for news of a loved one

Missing People Choir and Royal Mail Choir: 'I Hope'

Prayers for those who are missing *(led by clergy)*

Words of hope from a Missing People charity representative

Lighting of candles by families to remember those who are missing. *Light is taken from the pascal candle and distributed around the church and galleries above.*

Choir piece

Reading *(by one of the Missing People charity trustees)*

Congregational carol

Blessing

The order of service includes a central insert with photos of missing loved ones with personal messages to them from their families. All details of the charity are included. The service is publicized at The Connection at St Martin's, supporting people who are homeless, in the hope that there may be some clients who are missing who would want to come, or take the step of reconnecting to their families.

Where Love and Sorrow Meet

Samuel Wells

This is the only service in this book that took place as a one-off, rather than as part of an ongoing weekly, monthly or annual pattern. But it belongs here because it had a similar spirit to the other services outlined in this chapter. An occasion and an issue presented themselves – in this case the fiftieth anniversary of the Sexual Offences Act 1967, which began the process of decriminalizing gay sex in the UK, set within the context of the Church's emerging understanding of LGBT issues. A number of people who had campaigned around these issues and withstood prejudice and exclusion over many years approached St Martin's with a view to establishing an appropriate way to mark the anniversary. Together we explored what a service might look like and how it might set a tone around this commemoration and no doubt subsequent others.

We settled on the title 'Where Love and Sorrow Meet: A Service of Lament and Hope to Mark the Fiftieth Anniversary of the Sexual Offences Act 1967'. The theme of lament expressed the sadness and anger felt by many about all that had been lost to individuals, society and the Church in the neglect and rejection of a whole swathe of society that could have been such a blessing (and in many cases were, despite all odds), while the theme of hope expressed determination that the future would be better and brighter – but that much work and persuasion and advocacy remained to be done.

Six hundred people attended. The opening remarks of the service were as follows:

With regard to LGBTI identity, our country, culture and Church are on a slow journey from vilification and ostracism through tolerance and acceptance to celebration and blessing. This is a journey that's far from complete, but one that has had some key milestones: 1967 is one of those milestones. And so we've gathered to lament all that has been lost to God's Kingdom in the suppression, persecution and oppression of LGBTI people, to honour those whose courage and vision began the process of legislative and social change, to recognize that the Church has frequently been and in many senses still is a brake on that change and an attempt to put it into reverse rather than a driver or accelerator, and to offer a witness of hope for a future for country, culture and Church that more nearly resembles God's abundant, vibrant and glorious Kingdom.

Thank you for coming. We're glad you're here. I'm glad

you're here. Please stay for refreshments downstairs afterwards. And please know that, just by being here, you have witnessed to the triumph of God's grace and truth.

We all have different stories with God and understandings of what truth and holiness look like. I want us today to hold on to these central convictions: that God's imagination is diverse, beautiful and joyous; that bodily desire and love is precious, sanctifying and noble; and that in God the future is always bigger than the past.

We invited the London Gay Men's Chorus and it proved to be an inspired choice. The Chorus offered an immensely positive, collaborative, upbeat but playful spirit, and when it sang 'Bridge over troubled water' the familiar words had a more far-reaching resonance and moving depth. The use of two Jim Cotter hymns honoured a man who found joy in liturgical innovation while himself giving leadership to the LGBT movement in the Church. The sermon preached by Mark Oakley, on Mark's account of Jesus' baptism, was pivotal and included the following words concerning Jesus being baptized by John.

He gets pushed under the surface. You can only hear you under there, your own heart beating, and all the noise from the shore, the opinions, the dogmas, the criticisms and empty chatter all get drowned out. It's just him for a second or two and then, pulled out, he takes a deep breath of fresh air, a start to a newer life. We are told that he then hears a voice. Not from the shore but from heaven. This is the one voice that matters and it is tells him, 'You are mine, I love you, you make me happy.' Jesus then goes into a wilderness where all the empty voices come back at him, tempting and torturing his mind, trying to simmer him down out of the dignity he discovered by the water. In that desert he is learning to live up to the voice that matters, and not live down to the ones that don't, those that want to suffocate him. In Matthew's account, this included the devil endlessly quoting the Bible at him. Wild beasts and angels: you've met them both.

This story is in the deepest heartland of Christian faith. For

Christians, because of this story, water is thicker than blood. Baptism is where we hear the truth of who we are. Because of this story all the Scriptures are read to hear that love between the lines and any interpretation of the Bible where you cannot hear that voice of love is not to be trusted. When people use a text without some context it's usually a pretext for something else. The Bible is a record of people struggling, with mixed results, to believe that God loves people that I find it hard to. The truth of the waterside is the voice from God to each and every one: 'I've made you, look, you're beautiful, you make me happy, now, don't forget this even when they act like animals against you, even when you act like an animal because you're frightened.' When the Church believes this it works hard to ensure that in the ark every weird and wonderful creature has to budge up a bit to make a bit more space in the hay for another one.

Two key moments in the service were the Lament and the Litany of Honour, which are reproduced in full below. These were two ways in which all the emotions of the day were channelled into prayer and renewal.

Service outline

'Change is gonna come'

Greeting

Hymn: 'There's a wideness in God's mercy'

Lament

> Let us recognize before God how far the world is from the kingdom embodied in Christ.

> God of glory, in Isaiah you envisage how the wolf and the lamb may dwell together, but for so long your people have been reluctant to recognize your humanity in one another,

and even today people struggle to say to each other 'you are made this way because God wants one like you'; have mercy on your Church, turn hearts of stone into hearts of grace, and make all your people rejoice and sing.
God of glory
Have mercy on your Church.

God of abundance, in the Gospels you show Jesus giving your people more bread than they need, more wine than they can drink, more blessing than they can receive, but for so long your Church has failed to welcome the identities and gifts of so many of its people, and meanwhile experienced its life as scarcity; redeem the ministries of the rejected; shine through the witness of those whose truth must be heard; and infuse your Son's body on earth with the energy and blessing of the gifts it has for centuries despised.
God of abundance
Shower your people with your grace.

God of the rainbow, in the story of Noah you paint a world of diversity, suffering, restoration and new hope. Yet for countless generations your beloved children have had to hide who they are, pretend to be who they are not, deny those they love, betray others like themselves, and experience ostracism, contempt, violence and shame. And still there are many places where exclusion, diminishment and oppression are condoned, encouraged, applauded and perpetrated. Give your people courage to resist, wisdom to know how to respond, solidarity to stand together, inspiration to model a better way, and patience to endure until justice and mercy embrace.
God of the rainbow
Fill your Kingdom with justice and mercy.

God of resurrection, in whom the future is always bigger than the past, in Revelation you promise a time when you yourself will be with us, when you will wipe every tear from our eyes, when mourning and crying and pain will

be no more, and your Son will make all things new. Yet among your people there have been so many tears when there should have been celebration, so much mourning and crying and pain inflicted by the cruel on the innocent, and still today there are so many ways in which your children are downtrodden and patronized and demonized and under attack. Put a new song in our hearts, lift the voice of truth, bring the refining fire of your transformation, and let your glory roll like a never-failing stream.
God of resurrection
Let your glory roll like a never-failing stream. Amen.

Hebrew lament: El Malei Rachamim

Testimony: How it was

Litany of honour
Let us now praise God for those who have gone before us, who have made beauty out of fear, love out of rejection, grace out of cruelty and justice out of hatred.

For the forerunners on whose shoulders all those who know comparative freedom today gratefully stand
Hallowed be your name.

For W. H. Auden, Virginia Woolf, Oscar Wilde, E. M. Forster and all whose love dared not speak its name
Hallowed be your name.

For Benjamin Britten, John Gielgud, Angus McBean, Francis Bacon, Joe Orton, Alan Turing, Montague of Beaulieu, Peter Wildeblood and all those who bore the cost of public shame
Hallowed be your name.

For Sir John Wolfenden, Kenneth Robinson, Leo Abse, Humphrey Berkeley, A. E. (Tony) Dyson, Antony Grey, Doreen Cordell, Ted Wickham, John A. T. Robinson, Ian Dunn, Jackie Foster, Griff Vaughan-Williams, Sharley

MacLean, Michael Brown, Allan Horsfall and all who
contributed to the passing of the 1967 Act
Hallowed be your name.

For Freddie Mercury, Denholm Elliot, Ian Charleson,
Terrence Higgins, David Randall, Derek Jarman and all who
have carried the burden of AIDS
Hallowed be your name.

For Edward Carpenter, Jim Cotter, Peter Elers, Derek
Sherwin Bailey, Norman Pittenger, Una Kroll, Simon Bailey,
Michael De-la-Noy, Andrew Hallidie Smith, Derek Rawcliffe
and all who have shown your Church what being LGBTI
adds to being Christian
Hallowed be your name.

For the many who remain unnamed who were persecuted or
victimized because of their sexuality and were never able to
claim their full identity or to celebrate their love
Hallowed be your name.

For those who have taken their own life because they could
not live with those who could not live with them
Hallowed be your name.

For all who have worked for further changes to the law since
1967, and for those who have shown what a true society
looks like
Hallowed be your name.

For all who have campaigned for dignity and equality at cost
to their careers, reputations or livelihoods
Hallowed be your name.

For those who continue to face persecution and all who have
fled their home country because others could not live with
who they are
Hallowed be your name.

For all who despite setbacks and discouragements have
persevered and kept walking until the dawn
Hallowed be your name.

For all who have remained within the company of faith
despite being shunned, ostracized and shamed
Hallowed be your name.

Defend, O Lord, your servants with your heavenly grace;
uphold those who are downtrodden; empower those who
have truth to tell; restore any who are in despair; inspire all
who are beginning on a journey; and make your Church
more nearly resemble your Kingdom, now and for ever.
Amen.

Hymn: 'I vow to you my friends of earth' (Jim Cotter)

Reading

Sermon

Song: Mercy and judgement (Tracey Jones)

Prophecy: Living God's dream

Prophecy: The task ahead

Hymn: 'For all the saints' (Jim Cotter)

Intercessions

Chorus: 'Bridge over troubled water'

Blessing

Chorus: 'I sing the body electric'

3

On the Edge of the Year: Annual Special Services

Introduction

Most parishes have an annual round of significant services that transcend the conventional Sunday liturgy – whether because they draw in a wider circle of occasional worshippers, like Christmas and Easter, or hold a place in the common imagination, like Mothering Sunday and Harvest, or because they have a particular relevance to the context, like perhaps Rogation Sunday or the occasion of a Flower Festival or Annual Children's Holiday Club. St Martin-in-the-Fields has its own cycle of the congregational year and included in this chapter are some of its distinctive elements.

What each service outlined here has in common is a release – one might say eruption – of energy from quarters that often don't get heard when the weekly routine of 'getting the service prepared' and writing sermon and prayers and rehearsing music takes over. Within, around and beyond the congregation exists immense energy, creativity and interest, simply waiting to be approached, invited and given permission, guidance and affirmation to contribute untold riches. We find it unsustainable to make that a weekly or daily practice: instead we focus energies on particular occasions, of which the following are some.

Community Carol Service

Alastair McKay

St Martin-in-the-Fields has long held carol services that people travel from far and wide to attend. In the late 1980s, during the ministry of Geoffrey Brown, St Martin's wanted to build closer connections with local people and organizations. This coincided with a flourishing local business association, of which St Martin's became a part.

The Community Carols service was born with the aim of having a carol service specifically for 'the locals': those who lived and worked in the area around Trafalgar Square, and who might otherwise never come to a service at St Martin's, even though it was their local parish church. It was intended to build a sense of neighbourliness among those who were St Martin's neighbours. Over time this expanded to include a range of organizations with which St Martin's had developed relationships. This proved a fairly organic approach, and led to including many people and organizations from well beyond the physical parish. But the foremost intention remained to connect with local people and organizations. Hence among those who read lessons at the 2015 Community Carols were three people located on St Martin's very doorstep – a local *Big Issue* seller, the director of one of the national galleries, and a diplomat from one of the high commissions – along with the chief executive of the local business improvement district, and a senior Whitehall civil servant from the department where one of our churchwardens worked.

In 2016 we decided to take a more systematic approach to the Community Carols, by establishing which organizations were located within the parish. The aim was to connect more thoroughly organizations that are our immediate neighbours and within our parish boundary. The parish of St Martin-in-the-Fields is among a group of parishes in London known as 'explosion parishes'. These parishes have a relatively small resident population, but explode with people during the working week. St Martin's has only around 1,600 people resident in the parish – but over 42,000 working in the parish during the day-time.

The oddly shaped parish of St Martin's has three broad areas to it:

- Whitehall, from Parliament Square down to Trafalgar Square, consisting principally of government offices;
- three royal palaces and two royal parks, along with a few neighbouring streets off Pall Mall, mostly comprising offices; and
- the West End around Trafalgar Square, comprising a mixture of public and private organizations and enterprises.

Identifying the organizations located within St Martin's parish was a research project, and not a straightforward one. Initially I tried central and local government statistical sources, and the local business association, without getting the level of detail needed. In the end the most fruitful source proved to be Google Maps, at its highest level of magnification. I had to recognize that not all the information would be current. Ideally, this online search would have been backed up with on-the-ground visiting; but time limitations prevented this. (In a parish unlike St Martin's, with a locally resident congregation, parishioners might be recruited to help conduct such research.)

The research revealed that the parish of St Martin-in-the-Fields contains at least the following:

- three royal palaces and two royal parks
- the offices of 15 government departments, including No. 10 Downing Street
- 10 foreign embassies and tourism offices
- 28 hotels and apartment rental blocks
- 14 theatres and cinemas
- 8 museums and galleries, including 2 national galleries
- 11 national associations, institutes and societies
- the offices of 12 major national companies
- more than 90 shops, including many well-known retail chains, as well as speciality shops

- over 150 restaurants and cafes
- around 40 pubs, bars and nightclubs
- countless other offices of smaller companies and partnerships, including many in the creative industries.

The next challenge was trying to identify, where possible, a senior person in each of the organizations, along with an email address, so that a personalized invitation, signed by the Vicar, could be scanned and sent to them. This took persistence and creativity. In the event it proved unrealistic to identify such information for all the shops, restaurants, cafes, pubs and bars, so generic invitations were done for the their managers, which were distributed by hand.

The invitations included a reply deadline, and the suggestion of passing the invitation to a colleague if the invitee was unable to attend. In addition, invitees were asked to nominate a favourite carol. The letter indicated that some of the most popular and interesting carols would be incorporated within the service. This did not give a promise of inclusion, but it did increase the sense of participation, giving invitees a sense of contributing to the service. And all those who nominated a carol that was not chosen were named and thanked at the end of the service sheet, so that their contribution was at least marked. (Not everyone who accepted the invitation to attend chose to nominate a carol.)

The reply deadline enabled non-responders to be chased up a week before the deadline, and gave a cut off to nominations for the carols, so that the service could be planned and finalized in advance. It also meant that readers could be approached, from among the acceptees, who represented some of the diversity of organizations within the parish. (Several who were approached declined the invitation to be a reader, so finalizing the readers went down to the wire.) Seating was reserved in the church building for all named invitees who responded positively. And a more general invitation was sent out to all members of their organizations to attend the service.

A further crucial aspect of the welcome offered through the Community Carols service is the hospitality provided afterwards. St Martin's Cafe in the Crypt provides outstanding homemade mince pies, produced by our own pastry chef, along with mulled wine. This social time is the main opportunity for clergy and other church members to mingle with guests, build relationships and make connections, putting faces to names.

Each year a theme is chosen, to connect most of the carols and all of the readings, and to give a focus to the good news being shared. In 2016 the theme was 'Peace on Earth'. A short introductory sentence was provided before each reading, to help those attending see the thematic connection – since this might not be obvious to those without theological training, and since the readings went beyond the familiar Christmas ones.

Suitable carols were chosen from among the nominations, and others were included to make the most of the various choirs that participated. In 2016 these included the Northbank Community Choir, which draws people from organizations located in the area around St Martin's, and also three of St Martin's choirs: the Choral Scholars (aspiring professional singers on a year's scholarship), the Occasional Singers (a choir drawn mostly from the regular congregation), and the Children's Voices (a children's choir run by St Martin's).

The contacts made through the above research process then provided a list of people who could be contacted in the New Year to promote the range of events and opportunities available at St Martin's, at times other than the Advent and Christmas season.

Why are people drawn to a carol service? Often it's because of childhood associations sparked through familiar musical and narrative elements. We also believe those who come are looking for a sense of 'home' and belonging – of being incorporated into the great cast of characters welcoming the birth of the Christ child, and receiving the news of God's presence with us and among us. The approach to a Community Carols service taken here helps people to feel that they too are part of this great story.

This type of service communicates that St Martin's cares both about its sense of place, and those who are located within its locality, and does not take them for granted, but acknowledges that they make a valued contribution to our world. It also recognizes that although many may not be regular churchgoers, they may feel a connection with Christmas, perhaps only as a social or cultural event; but perhaps also because it speaks to a deeper yearning which they may otherwise not have articulated, a longing to connect with God. The collection taken during the service goes towards the BBC Radio 4 St Martin-in-the-Fields Christmas Appeal, which works with those who are homeless or facing homelessness. Not only is there an important connection with the Christmas story, but it gives those attending a chance to show that they too care for those who are homeless on the streets of Westminster, and that they too want to make a difference in their lives.

Together, all of these elements contribute to the joy and delight of the evening.

Service outline

Theme: Peace on Earth

Carol while people are taking their seats: 'Go tell it on the mountain' *(sung by the Northbank Community Choir)*

Welcome

Carol 1: 'Once in royal David's city' *(verse 1 solo, sung by one the Children's Voices; carol nominated by a senior civil servant)*

Introduction to the first reading: The Psalmist writes of God's promised anointed one, who will come and bring justice to a fallen and chaotic world.

Reading 1: Psalm 2 *(read by a high commissioner)*

Carol 2: 'O little town of Bethlehem' *(carol nominated by the director of a national society, a theatre manager and a senior officer of a major cinema group)*

Introduction to the second reading: Isaiah, a prophet writing in the eighth century BC, promises the arrival of a child who will establish a kingdom of justice and peace.

Reading 2: Isaiah 9.2–7 *(read by a senior member of one of the royal households)*

Carol 3: 'O radiant dawn' (MacMillan) *(sung by the Choral Scholars)*

Introduction to the third reading: Luke's account tells of the birth of Jesus, the promised anointed one, whose arrival announces the coming of peace on earth.

Reading 3: Luke 2.1–14 *(read by the chief executive of a national music company)*

Carol 4: 'Star candles' (Michael Head) *(sung by the Children's Voices)*

Introduction to the fourth reading: The apostle Paul explains the significance of Jesus' death on the cross, which brings about peace between human beings and God, and between people.

Reading 4: Ephesians 2.13–20 *(read by a director of a national society)*

Carol 5: 'Silent night' *(first verse in German, sung by the Choral Scholars; carol nominated by the chief executive of a national academy; the general manager of an entertainment venue; and the director of a national gallery, in memory of a colleague who had died earlier in the year)*

Introduction to the fifth reading: John, a Christian disciple imprisoned on the island of Patmos, offers a vision of the eternal city where peace is finally realized.

Reading 5: Revelation 22.1–6, 16–17 *(read by a senior civil servant)*

Carol 6: 'In the bleak midwinter' *(carol nominated by the secretary of a members' club; the park manager of two Royal Parks; and the chief executive of a national music company)*

Carol 7: 'Away in a manger' *(Basque tune, sung by the Children's Voices; carol nominated by the president of a national teaching association)*

Prayers led by the Vicar

The Lord's Prayer

Carol 8: 'O holy night' *(sung by the Choral Scholars and Occasional Singers; carol nominated by a senior research fellow of a national institute; and the curator of a small national museum)*

Carol 9: 'O come, all ye faithful' *(carol nominated by the general manager of a major hotel; and a high commissioner)*

Blessing

Carol 10: 'Hark! the herald angels sing'

Organ voluntary

(60 minutes in total)

Note on inside back cover: 'We are also grateful for carol nominations from [extensive list of names and roles]. Sadly it wasn't possible to incorporate all the diverse nominations.'

Christmas Crib Service

Richard Carter

Each Christmas Eve we hold a Crib Service at St Martin-in-the-Fields. It is a chance to tell the Christmas story to a wide range of families, children and others who perhaps do not come to church that often. I wanted to dramatize the story and make it come alive, in a way that not only engages the audience but is also relevant to our times. The Christmas nativity is probably more dramatized than any other story – so much so that it can easily lose its power, becoming more of a traditional fairy tale in which parents can watch their offspring perform in angel, sheep or donkey costumes, or with tea towels on their heads. Alternatively, if we go for greater authenticity, it can seem traditional but trite, too familiar or tame. How can we create a nativity that not only moves and delights, but also challenges and disturbs? How do we tell the Christmas story in a way that excites us to hope and joy? What are the dramatic elements we can use to make this story come alive to an audience of all ages and all walks of life?

The medieval mystery cycles still have genuine vibrancy and drama. They bring the gospel narratives down to earth, root them in flesh and blood humanity, and are not frightened to tease, shock or outrage. How to capture something of that earthy irreligious Spirit to tell the story of this most holy night? I decided to use rhyming couplets. This offers a form that can amuse, but also pushes the writer to find words, expressions and allusions that make the story come alive for today. I also wanted a way I could encourage audience participation, in the tradition of Christmas pantomime, and, while capturing the attention of children, also involve the adults in the audience, in the way good, modern, animated films have done. I deliberately choose a cast that draws in the whole congregation and write a script that can involve both adults and children. As time for rehearsal before Christmas is hard to find, I employ a form that is manageable with limited rehearsal time and is held together by two narrators, who can use scripts. I encourage the actors to learn their parts by heart, which makes the performance come alive. This nativity has been performed not only at St Martin's but in schools, both primary and secondary, where it has been greatly enjoyed, with both students and staff taking part. Each year I have added contemporary references to keep the script up to date. Part of the enjoyment of this script is that it can be adapted, and new rhymes invented, to respond to current events. The couplets have the ability, it seems, to weave their way round people's defences, and perhaps offer a radical challenge to our present times – as the original birth narratives in Matthew and Luke do, and as does, most astonishingly of all, the incarnation itself.

The script is broken into four main parts:

- the Poem of God's Love for the World
- the Poem of the Stable
- the Poem of the Shepherds and Angels
- the Poem of the Kings.

These parts can also be played independently of each other. In our dramatization during the blessing of the crib in Trafalgar Square we have used the Poem of the Stable, and for our Radio 4 Sunday worship we have used the Poem of the Shepherds and Angels. Each of these parts is held together by carols and music, chosen to accord with the particular part of the story. At St Martin's we are blessed with wonderful choirs and singers to assist us. Thus the shepherds in the fields have been greeted by bursts of the Hallelujah Chorus and the most wonderful tap-dancing angel from our Children's Club. Mary and Joseph have sung adaptations of Leonard Bernstein's 'There's no place for us' and later 'O holy night' – sung as a trio, with the Angel Gabriel joining in from the pulpit. At the same time this drama is not dependent on having brilliant singers; it could just as well use carols and children's voices.

It is vital to get the audience involved before you begin. You can practise the lines they must shout out and insist the nativity depends on them.

Wake up, wake up, I need help now
My wife's having a baby and we don't know how.
Wake up! Wake up! Can't you see?
God depends on you and me.
He's come to save both rich and poor
Open your hearts, open the door!

Casting is very important. I choose a young child to play the part of God and have both male and female shepherds. Parts are included for younger members too. The most important part, of course, is the baby Jesus. Jesus needs to be a real baby boy or girl. The church sanctuary becomes the stable; Mary and Joseph move behind the altar for the birth. Joseph describes the birth.

It was as though God bent down heaven to this stable drawn
And the child that came was love new born.

At this moment the baby is lifted up by both Mary and Joseph
from behind the altar. It makes the congregation gasp, because
no one is expecting a real child. Parents are usually delighted
to have their offspring play the part of Jesus, as long as they
are kept at hand to become Mary-surrogates should the child
become in any way distressed. One year our baby, though deliv-
ered on time, was running a temperature on the day, so we had
to find a new baby from the audience. We were fortunate! Sometimes the baby is more than three months old and looks a bit big
to be newborn. In such circumstances Mary can add the lines:

See my child, so beautiful and wise
He's the Son of God, which explains his size!

I do hope you will perform this nativity, which is why it is
included here. Just let us know at St Martin's and we will be glad
to give permission. I know you will have a lot of fun performing
it. We hope it will make your congregation both laugh and weep;
but, most important, make them think how this nation would
welcome the Christ child today.

Script

Carol: 'O come, all ye faithful'

Welcome

The Poem of God's Love for the World

Narrator 1   God sat on her throne in heaven
               You see she was the boss
               and all the people down on earth
               had made her rather cross.
               God I'm tired of all the war and hate

They'd better change, it's getting late.
They've spoilt the planet, burnt the trees
Melted the ice caps into the seas.
Everyone in the world is my son or daughter
I don't want the earth I created under water
If only they would follow my law
Instead of always going to war.
In Syria and Iraq my children cry
Stop the killing or we all will die
So many refugees on the roam
No safety, no country no place to call home
I see a world so full of pain
And there's always someone else to blame.
Religion was never meant to divide but to reveal
your Saviour
And show you how to love your neighbour.
There is so much suffering, don't you care?
I made this world with enough to share
I want a world of love and peace,
A world where joy will never cease.
What can I do, what shall be done?
I think I'll have to send my son.
This tiny baby will make them weep
He will pull down the proud and raise up the
meek.

Narrator 2   In the sixth month the angel Gabriel was sent by
God to a town in Galilee called Nazareth, to a
virgin engaged to a man whose name was Joseph
of the house of David. The virgin's name was
Mary.

The Poem of Mary and Joseph

Mary   My soul magnifies the Lord
And my spirit rejoices in the God who called.
It was early in the morning, at first I thought I
dreamed
As through my door the light of heaven streamed

I was full of fear and sat up in bed
And saw an angel with golden wings and a halo of
fire around her head
Her clothes were white, as bright as bright can be
And with her finger she pointed at me
And then I saw a dove flying free
And I felt God's love as deep as the sea.

Gabriel   Mary! Mary! Greetings favoured one
The Lord is with you and a new life has begun
Do not be afraid, Mary, this is your call
That you will have a son who will be the Saviour
of all.

Mary   How can this be? This must be a joke
But this really is the truth of things;
I've never been with a bloke
And what about my fiancé Joseph? What will he
say?
It won't look good on my wedding day.

Gabriel   I know it sounds hard to believe
But by the power of the Holy Spirit you will conceive
And God said it would really please us
If you gave him the Christian name of Jesus!

Mary   *(to herself)* Why me, what's this for?
He could have chosen the rich rather than the poor
An unmarried mother is not an easy thing to be
They'll shout and curse and want to stone me
So why is it that in my heart I feel such joy
And long to be the mother of this little boy?
(to Gabriel) If he is to be the saviour of all
I must have the courage to answer God's call.
Despite my worries I feel no dread
I am the servant of the Lord, let it happen as God
has said.
Joseph! Joseph! I've got something you should
know
I'm afraid it may come as a terrible blow
Look, this is really hard to say,
you see I'm having a baby on Christmas Day!

Joseph	Jesus Christ! What's your game?
Mary	How did you know that's his name?
Joseph	What do you mean? How could this be?

You've always been so true to me.
I don't want to leave but I just feel so sad
I simply can't believe that God is the Dad
I feel all my trust has been totally blown
I just need some time on my own ...
(Joseph walks away and then ponders)

Joseph   How could she do this? She had always been so true
I didn't want to be a monster but what can I do?
So I kept it quiet, fortunately there were no tabloids in this age
Because an immaculate conception would have made the front page.
I was so confused I wanted to die
And I just couldn't believe that Mary would lie.
It's not at all like the traditions of my youth
But then we live in the age of post-truth
And then I slept and had a dream.
(music begins)

God   Joseph! Joseph! Don't be afraid to take Mary as your wife
She's the best thing you've ever had in your life
You have been given a calling to something much higher
So marry Mary, mother of the Messiah.

Joseph   I was filled with hope by the wonder of that dream
And realized that things are not always what they seem.
I knew that a mother she would soon be
But the mother of God – that was news to me.
Mary! Mary have no fear,
If you'll still have me I'm still here!

Mary and Joseph (sing)
There's a place for us, somewhere God's place for us.

Peace and quiet and open air wait for us
somewhere.
There's a time for us, someday a time for us,
Time together with time to share,
Time to learn, time to care, someday! Somewhere.
We'll find a new way of living,
We'll find a way of forgiving
Somewhere ...
There's a place for us, a time and place for us.
Hold my hand and we're halfway there.
Hold my hand and I'll take you there somehow,
someday, somewhere!

Carol: 'Once in royal David's city'

The Poem of the Stable

Narrator 1   This is how the birth of Jesus took place.
The Emperor Augustus came out with this decree
That everyone should register their names in their
home towns wherever that may be.
In those days, everyone in Europe had to do what
the Emperors say
They had far more power than Theresa May.

Narrator 2   Now Mary and Joseph went to Bethlehem but it
was not an easy ride.
It made Mary and Joseph wonder if God was
really on their side
The economy of the Roman Empire had also been
in decline
So trying to call an ambulance was a waste of time.
Mary was in urgent need of medical care but no
one realized
Like an omen for the future if the NHS gets
privatized.

Narrator 1   When they reached Bethlehem every place was
filled to the brim
Mary was ready to deliver and things were looking
grim.

	Even if Joseph had spent weeks on the internet browsing
	It was impossible to find any affordable housing.
Narrator 2	The rents in Bethlehem had rocketed
	Which unscrupulous landlords pocketed.
	You see though King Herod claimed to care
	Like Donald Trump he cared much more for his hair
	He thought he was the most powerful man in charge
	He depended on sycophants like Nigel Farage
	And opposition lived in fear and held no sway
	Like the Labour Party it had melted away.
Narrator 1	But this is Mary and Joseph and this their story
	People like you and me, not those of wealth or glory.
	Christ came among us I'll tell you how
	It happened then, it's still happening now.
Joseph	I'm worried about Mary, I love her to bits
	But the thought of her in pain sends me out of my wits.
	Out in the streets people just walk past us or stare
	No one in this city really seems to care.
	Wake up! Wake up! I need help now!
	My wife's having a baby and we don't know how!
	Wake up! Wake up! Does no one hear?
	She's ready to deliver … the birth is near.
Innkeeper 1	Who's that knocking at the door of my inn?
	It's far too late to make such a din!
	I've got my boyfriend in here; and dinner is waiting
	I don't want to worry about my TripAdvisor rating!
Mary	Please everyone will you help Joseph shout?
Joseph	Wake up! Wake up! I need help now!
	My wife's having a baby and we don't know how!
All	Wake up! Wake up! Can't you see
	God depends on you and me.
	He's come to save both rich and poor
	Open your hearts open the door!

LITURGY ON THE EDGE

Innkeeper 1	We're full every room, no place to stay
	Now stop banging on my door and go away!
Joseph	Wake up! Wake up! I need help now!
	My wife's having a baby and we don't know how!
All	Wake up! Wake up! Can't you see
	God depends on you and me!
	He's come to save both rich and poor
	Open your hearts open the door.
Innkeeper 2	Stop banging on my door, unless you cease
	I'm going to have to call the police.
	What are you, homeless? A down and out or
	refugee?
	Go home! Go home! It's nearly three!
Joseph	Wake up! Wake up! I need help now!
	My wife's having a baby and we don't know how!
All	Wake up! Wake up! Can't you see
	God depends on you and me!
	He's come to save both rich and poor
	Open your hearts open the door.
Joseph	Please let us in ... for the love of God.
Innkeeper 2	Having a baby, how irresponsible, they should put
	you in jail
	I've read about scroungers like you in the *Daily*
	Mail
	Don't think I am going to provide you with a
	holiday chalet
	Because they've thrown you out of your filthy
	camp in Calais!
	I bet the Roman Empire gives you benefits, I know
	what the facts is
	And it's people like me who has to pay for you
	from my taxes.
	A mother indeed! You're not fit to stay
	When the baby is born, they'll take it away.
Innkeeper 1	Harold you're such a terrible snob
	You've ripped off your tenants so much you've
	never needed a job.

82

82

Have a heart, the poor lass is pregnant and in a
terrible fix
I know what it's like, you've given me six.
The suffering of homeless people in this city is
really chronic
Perhaps you can think about them instead of your
next gin and tonic.

Innkeeper 2 You know you're such a soft touch
Give these migrants an inch and they'll take too
much
We need to protect our own interests that's my call
Shut them out and build a wall!
So you can tell this suspicious couple where to go
When it comes to helping people like this I'm
voting NO.

Mary O Joseph I'm exhausted, what's to be done
I need a place to rest, to give birth to our son?

Mary and Joseph (sing)
There's no place for us, nowhere a single space for
us.
Peace and quiet and an open door wait for us
nowhere.
There's no place for us, not even a single space for
us,
Nowhere to go and nowhere to stay, no one to
help, no one to pay, nowhere
No way. We'll find a way of surviving. God'll find
a way of providing
Somehow, somewhere.
There is God with us – a gift of love inside of us.
Hold on my child we're nearly there.
Hold on my child and I'll take you there somehow,
someway, somewhere.
(music continues)

Innkeeper Look you two, if you really need a bed
There's no place left but a cattle shed.
There's an ox in there, an ass and some chickens
too

	It's not a maternity unit, more like a zoo.
Joseph	A stable is fine for the time has come
	For Mary to give birth to God's only son.
Narrator 2	While they were in Bethlehem, the time came for
	Mary to deliver her child. And she gave birth to
	her first-born son and wrapped him in bands of
	cloth. And laid him in a manger because there was
	no place for them in the inn.
Joseph	So a stable, with an ox and an ass looking on that
	was our lot
	But this child was coming ready or not
	It was the miracle, the miracle of a birth
	That seemed to unite both heaven and earth.
	It was as though God bent down, heaven to this
	stable drawn
	And the child that came was love new born
	All the darkness melted away
	And we were filled with the light of Christmas Day.
	Look! Look! God held in her hands so full of joy
	Praise God! Praise God for this little boy!
Mary	Look at the light around his head
	He is even more beautiful than the angels said.
God	This is my son, come and see –
	In fact they say he looks just like me.

Children's Voices: 'Lullaby for Baby Jesus' (Brazilian trad.)

Carol: 'Silent night'

The Poem of the Shepherds and Angels

Narrator 2	In the region there were shepherds living in the
	fields keeping watch over their flock by night …
God	Angels in heaven wake up! No time to lose!
	You've got to go and take some good news
	A baby's born in Bethlehem
	You must go and welcome him.
Narrator 2	So the angels took off, what a sight

All wearing white and shining bright.
The lightning flashed, the thunder boomed
As round and round the earth they zoomed.

Shepherd 1 Now down on the earth around the sheepfold
We shepherds were sitting tired and cold
We'd just been having our shepherd's staff meeting
we would have preferred some central heating.

Shepherd 2 A cup of hot tea would have been nice
Because my toes had turned to ice.
Far from town with no text messages or mobile phone
I was having a bit of a moan
No food to eat and no all-night stores
And no way to hear the latest football scores.

Shepherd 3 Shepherds can also feel rather bitter
When they feel they're missing out onWhatsApp and Twitter
Nothing to put on my Facebook page
And not even earning a living wage.

Shepherd 2 All politicians always want our votes?
But the real problem is we've got no coats
With zero-hour contracts it's hard to live your dreams
And all we get at the food banks is tins of baked beans.

Shepherd 1 So we blew in our gloves to warm our hands
And wondered if the government believed in their Brexit plans.
Shepherds come from far and wide, and need free movement of labour
Because no one wants to do this job unless you love your neighbour.
In terms of our workers' rights no one gives a damn
As long as for their Sunday lunch they get their English roast lamb.

Shepherd 2 I think that God no longer cares
I'm not even going to bother to say my prayers

	I'm homeless on these hills all night and my life is really frugal
	I haven't learnt the tax dodges of Amazon, Starbucks and Google.
Shepherd 4	Dad, you're always complaining, I'm tired of your moans
	Christmas is coming I can feel it in my bones.
	Look Dad! Look Dad! Look what's that up high?
	Like angels of light that dance across the sky.
Narrator 2	Suddenly there was a flash of light
	And the world was lit up all flaming bright
	Was it a new day dawning?
	Or was it the result of global warming?
	From the top of their heads to the tip of their toes
	They felt the Holy Spirit glow.
	And suddenly they heard a heavenly band
	Singing praises to God with outstretched hands.
Narrator 1	And all the sheep went:
All	Baa baa baa!
Narrator 1	And all the angels cried:
All	Alleluia!
Angel (sings)	Hallelujah Chorus
Shepherds	Who are you? Are you a ghost?
Angel	No, I'm part of the Heavenly Host!
Shepherd 1	I see only a blinding light
	It must be God! Wow, what a sight!
Shepherd 2	Tell us angels what is your song
	By which you make my whole heart long?
Narrator 1	And all the sheep went:
All	Baa baa baa!
Narrator 1	And all the angels cried:
All	Alleluia!
Angel	Hallelujah Chorus
Narrator 2	It was a message from God that Gabriel began to sing
	As all the angels flapped their wings.
Gabriel	Don't be frightened, please don't worry
	But to Bethlehem you must hurry.

	Tonight is full of peace and joy
	Because tonight is born a little boy
	And you will find this baby sweet
	In a stable fast asleep
	This little baby sleeping curled
	Will be the Saviour of the world.
Narrator 1	Then suddenly the heavenly hosts
	praised Father, Son and Holy Ghost
	And all the angels began to yell:
	Emmanuel! Emmanuel!
	And all the sheep went:
All	Baa baa baa!
Narrator 2	And the angels cried:
All	Alleluia!
Angel	Hallelujah Chorus
Shepherd 4	Princes are born in hospitals or palaces as a rule
	But a Prince born for us, in a stable, wow that's so cool!
Shepherd 5	I went to the stable and saw where the baby Jesus lay
	In a manger filled with hay.
	He didn't have any Christmas presents and I thought that was quite shocking
	So I gave him my lamb to put in his stocking.
Narrator 1	And all the sheep went:
All	Baa baa baa!
Narrator 1	And the angels cried:
All	Alleluia!
Angel	Hallelujah Chorus finale
Mary	*(sung)* O holy night the stars are brightly shining
	It is the night of my dear baby's birth.
	Long lay the world in sin and error pining
	Till he appeared and my soul felt its worth.
Mary and Joseph	
	A thrill of hope the weary world rejoices
	For yonder breaks a new glorious morn.
Angel	Fall on your knees. O hear the angels' voices.

All   O night divine, O night when Christ was born, O
night divine, O night O night divine.

Carol: 'While shepherds watched their flocks by night'

The Poem of the Kings

Narrator 1 In a land far away
Where hot winds blow and palm trees sway
Sipping sherbet around the bar
Were Caspar, Melchior and Balthasar.
These three sat all night and tried to see
What the strange sign in the sky could be
For in the darkness a star had pierced the night
Flashing, astonishing, shining bright.

Caspar   Where has it come from and what can it mean?
Is it a vision or a dream?

Melchior We must follow this star like a road of light
Through wind and rain, day and night.

Balthasar Forget it Melch, let's stay here
I think its meaning's far from clear.

Caspar   No, no, this one is for real my boy
It seems to fill my heart with joy
It seems to speak of peace and life
An end to wars with gun or knife.

Melchior The ancient books and stories told
Of a Saviour born to save the world.
I want to find the truth of this
It's a truth we really mustn't miss.

Page boy Dad, can I come too? I can give you a hand
And bring my iPad to play in the sand.
And if we find the Saviour that will be so neat
Think of all the people I'll be able to tweet.

Narrator 2 They set off following the star, without even a map
And it was a long way through the desert without
a tap.

Caspar   I think camels are great but not every day
To sit on a hump and feel it sway.

Melchior	Without a bath or toilet it's not much fun
	And no cold water to cool my tongue.
Balthasar	With sand storms and heat and many falls
	I'd rather dance gangnam style with chubby Ed
	Balls.
Page boy	It's such a long way, and Christmas is on Sunday
	And we're using camels not a new Heathrow
	runway.
Kings	Don't you think we've come too far?
All	NO! NO! FOLLOW THE STAR!
Narrator 1	You missed it.
Kings	Don't you think we've come too far?
All	NO! NO! FOLLOW THE STAR!
Caspar	We must have faith, don't look back,
	Follow this star along the track.
Balthasar	I'm hot and sore, what a fool!
	I should have stayed by the swimming pool.
Page boy	I wish I was playing with my Xbox
	Instead of all this sand in my socks.
	At first we were having such fun
	But now I'm beginning to miss my mum.
Kings	Don't you think we've come too far?
All	NO! NO! FOLLOW THE STAR!
Balthasar	Finally we reached Jerusalem full of hope
	Dreaming of a soft bed and a bath with soap.
Melchior	We met King Herod and asked him straight
	But I saw his eyes were full of hate.
Kings	Where is the baby born to be
	The king of the Jews to set us free?
Herod	Where will the Messiah be born?
Narrator 2	In the town of Bethlehem for this is what the
	prophets wrote: 'you are by no means the least of
	the cities for from you will come a king who will
	guide my people Israel.'
Herod	What! what! Do you think this is something they
	are free to choose?
	I, King Herod, am the king of the Jews
	King of the Jews! Look at my face

I'm the only king in this place.
In Bethlehem make a careful search for this
imposter king
(Then I will tear him limb from limb)
This little baby is no match for me
I, King Herod, will kill him, wait and see!

Kings   Don't you think we've come too far?

All   NO! NO! FOLLOW THE STAR!

Narrator 1   So at last in Bethlehem they found a stable where
the baby lay
A baby who took their breath away
And his mother by his side
When she saw the wise men cried:

Mary   You are welcome here tonight
Beneath this star so shining bright.
I know this little child will be
The Saviour born to set you free.
Did you hear the Angels tell?
He is Emmanuel, Emmanuel!

Page boy   Wow look at the baby's face it shines so bright
And fills this stable with his light
Look at his tiny fingers and tiny toes
How God made him nobody knows.
I do not know why or how
But I know that God is with us now.

Narrator 1   So when you think how lost you are:

All   ALWAYS! ALWAYS! FOLLOW THE STAR!

Carol: 'We three kings'

Prayers

Carol: 'Away in a manger'

Blessing of the Crib

Carol: 'Hark! the herald-angels sing'

Palm Sunday

Richard Carter

Worship and drama are not simply two distinct elements that form a useful analogy. Drama is essential to the life of worship at many levels. Prior to any formulated creed, doctrine or organized concept of church, Christ left his witnesses with the memory of a drama performed in the world: vivid sense impressions scorched upon their minds and bodies so that they could never forget. It was these events that the disciples would continue to live out and live out of, replaying the memories over and over again in the spiral of their own lives. This anamnesis would become the foundation of the liturgy that would involve making those events part of the present, as they witnessed to all those who did not know Christ:

> We declare to you what was from the beginning, what we have heard, what we have seen with our eyes, what we have looked at and touched with our hands, concerning the word of life – this life was revealed, and we have seen it and testify to it. (1 John 1.1–2)

The description we find in 1 John is physical. It is not a theological concept but a man of flesh and blood to whom they witness. The challenge for them was not simply to make sense of the life of Christ but for his life to make sense of their own lives and calling. The drama they recalled was not over yet and it was they themselves who had been called to take up the roles Christ had given them in the final act. It was Christ's own drama that would live on within the liturgy of the Church. In the dramatic reading and remembrance of that saving event,

> we are invited to identify ourselves in the story being contemplated, to re-appropriate who we are now, and who we shall or can be, in terms of the story. Its movements, transactions, transformations become *ours*: we take responsibility for this or that position within the narrative.[1]

---

1 Rowan Williams, *On Christian Theology*, Oxford: Blackwell, 2000, p. 50.

The craft of drama itself, stripped of pretension, is the art of bringing a narrative to life: 'Basically you are telling a story ... You are trying to tell the story well, clearly, vividly, in a way that will increase the vitality of everyone concerned.'[2] In this act of telling the story can become inextricably linked with the story of those to whom it is told.

In Greek the word 'drama' means *action*. Drama is not simply a form of literature, 'the event itself stands in the place of text'.[3] What makes drama lies beyond the words it uses, it has to be embodied, it has to be seen in action and acted out.[4] The medium of drama is the flesh. Likewise the 'Word of God' is not simply spoken word, it is the Word which becomes flesh and dwells among us. The incarnation involves all the five senses. Incarnation is drama. The Word made flesh speaks through the flesh. The face, the body, the voice, the life, the movement, the humanity, the need, the joy, the thirst, the sweat, the pain – in fact everything about Christ mediates the divine through his body. And the response to Christ is also physical. We *re-member* him through the memory of the body, through sight, sound, taste, smell, touch, intellect, feeling and intuition. 'Bodies are shaped memory.'[5] It is through the flesh, the body, that the full communication between God and human beings begins. Chauvet writes that, while we cannot negate the intellectual approach to understanding Christ, neither can we see it as the only method of initiation into the Christian faith: 'There is no other way of entering into the mystery of Christ than to allow oneself to be grasped by it. To be initiated is not to have learned truths to believe but to have received a tradition, in a way, through the pores of one's skin.'[6]

---

2 Peter Brook, *Between Two Silences: Talking with Peter Brook*, London: Methuen, 2000, p. 14.

3 Brook, *The Empty Space*, p. 55.

4 See Martin Esslin, *An Anatomy of Drama*, London: Temple Smith, 1976, pp. 14ff.

5 Stephen Buckland, 'Ritual Bodies and "Cultural Memory"', *Concilium*, 'Liturgy and the Body', 1995/3, p. 52.

6 Louis-Marie Chauvet, 'The Liturgy in its Symbolic Space', *Concilium*, 'Liturgy and the Body', 1995/3, p. 31.

In the Passion drama it is Jerusalem that becomes the stage for the final conflict. And Christ makes one of the most dramatic entrances in history. He rides a donkey into the centre of the 'Holy City', into the very place where he knows he will face his greatest opposition, betrayal and death. On this stage all the major characters in the drama are gathered for the finale: Christ and his confused disciples follow him into this final storm; the women who have followed him from Galilee and will become witnesses of both death and resurrection; his mother Mary; his betrayer Judas; his opposition including the chief priests, elders and Pharisees, even Nicodemus will be there; the Roman secular authorities, including their vacillating governor, centurions and soldiers; and of course the fickle crowd capable of becoming both worshippers and lynch mob. No theatrical director could conceive of a more dramatic convergence of events than this final week in Christ's life, which will become the source of all our future dramas of redemption.

The last days in anyone's life become highly charged and significant. Meetings, actions, last words will be focused upon and recalled and reflected upon after the death. Christ leaves words branded upon the collective memory, but also powerful actions and symbols which will be endlessly meditated and reflected upon. The renowned theatre director Peter Brook believes that a true symbol is hard and clear, it cuts ever deeper, it explodes through the crust and appearance of our world so that we see the molten lava of creation at work. Look at Christ's symbols and symbolic action in this his final week: a donkey, palm branches, overthrowing money-changers' tables, washing feet, bread, wine, a dark night of prayer, a kiss, silence, a tortured body, a courtyard fire and a cock crowing, a king falling under the weight of a cross, nails hammered through flesh, three crosses on a hill, bitter wine, death cries, the flow of blood and water, darkness covering the earth, a borrowed tomb, a stone rolled away, an empty tomb, a garden, an encounter with someone who had died, a locked room, a road, broken bread. What more powerful symbols could there be than this drama for ever held in the human psyche? These symbols and this drama will become the liturgy on the edge – the liturgy that focuses and embodies the memories we pass on and live out. We tell Christ's story and Christ tells ours.

The church itself provides the stage for this drama. After all it was what it was designed for. The pulpit where the people are addressed by Pilate, the stalls where the high priests take their seats, the altar – the place of sacrifice and judgement – and the cross in the east window, the place of death and also the place of hope. In our church we are called to make use of this space, to use its beauty and the powerful visual symbols and sense of the sacred it contains. We need to break away from the static and the tokenistic and restore a sense that this is the place of revelation and transfiguration.

In our Passion Drama we need to find a Jesus who will speak to our time. Each actor who takes up this role will bring something different to add: a new vantage point, a new way of seeing Christ. In choosing the person to play Christ this is our challenge: to make Christ the character of transformation. It is so easy in a dramatization for Jesus to become the passive victim and for Judas and the conspiracy against him to dominate. Somehow we must find a Jesus who will hold centre stage and whose violent death changes everything, including we who witness.

One year I asked Fiona MacMillan to play Jesus. Fiona is among the contributors to this book. She chairs our Disability Advisory Group. Fiona has always had a presence. Her voice combines both sensitivity and authority, and though her wheelchair grounds her and reveals her disability it in no way contains her. It becomes, as it were, the stage for her ability: part of the expression of one whose struggle has unbound her and given her insight and a voice for others. For those of us who worked with her, as we rehearsed the Passion Narrative, we became acutely aware of the very meaning of movement and mobility and what it means, how easy it is to assume freedom of movement and take it for granted, and how easy it is to invade the space of another, taking over, assuming, prejudging rather than recognizing. Yet, as we grow in awareness we begin to perceive that in what we thought of as restriction there can be an even greater freedom, the freedom of being who you are, the authenticity of acknowledging our human limitations and yet at the same time the authority of a humanity and a spirit that cannot be constricted and somehow becomes more obviously unimprisonable. We see this Spirit in Christ who, though bound, is in fact the most unbound and, though nailed to a cross, is in fact freer than all his persecutors.

Fiona described the experience in this way:

I wasn't at all keen to play Jesus. I always instinctively trust Richard but questioned him quite vigorously as to why he'd asked me. Richard patiently explained what it was and what it would involve, and was continuously reassuring. I knew it would be a big statement to have someone in a wheelchair portraying Jesus. It was important for me to spend time exploring how this might truly be symbolism rather than tokenism. And what the cost might be for me. I am used to being on the edge. My usual place is tucked under the pulpit and behind a pillar on the darker, quieter side of church. Coming into the middle would on its own mean moving into a more difficult place, making myself more vulnerable and exposed. To not only come to the centre but to stand behind the altar, to portray Jesus in the depths of his torment and vulnerability felt too enormous, and I felt unequal to the task. But I trusted Richard, and said yes, while keenly aware of my own inadequacy.

Saying Jesus' words out loud was difficult, even when alone at home. The words are so resonant with meaning, with the well-known story that follows, that to be the one who was saying them was overwhelming. To say them out loud in church was utterly exposing, every time, even though they felt very different as I began to hear them from the inside. As a neurologically impaired wheelchair user I always have to learn how to move in new spaces. I spent time working out movements with Richard, learning how and where to move and seeing how my body would respond. Particular sounds or movements triggered spasms. Some I tried to suppress, others I simply had to go with or endure. We found uses for some of them – like vocal tics when being whipped, or arm spasms when being crucified. We moved, practised lines, learned how to get up steps sideways, how to lean on the altar to look as though I was standing for the Last Supper, when I would need support and how it worked to be supported – what would enable and what would stop me being able to continue. It was all in the detail.

Then we rehearsed with others. At the beginning of the first rehearsal I tried to explain to the cast about my conditions and my symptoms. I hoped that as they got used to my involuntary movements and tics I would relax and hopefully be a bit less symptomatic. It felt like coming out. In rehearsal we learnt alongside each other and became a team. I'd already been rehearsing so had a head start. I remembered movements easily because I always have to learn new spaces; I'd learned my lines so was able to give cues and hold things together. People started to follow me because I knew what I was doing – I had disciples! I began to feel responsible for them. I knew what was coming when they didn't. I began to inhabit the words, and to imagine what others might be feeling. I began to feel compassion – for the disciples who were trying but not really understanding, and especially for the guards, who were becoming increasingly uneasy about causing pain.

I hardly slept the night before and was questioning why it had ever felt like a good idea to expose myself and my weakness so publicly, and how on earth I was physically going to get through. Arriving, I simply had to let go and be fully present as things unfolded. Much as I might not want to be there and didn't feel prepared or worthy, it was what was going to happen. I took my place with the disciples at the front of the church, in the middle – and we took a leap of faith together.

There was something deeply horrifying about seeing someone in a wheelchair mocked and humiliated and tortured by her accusers. It alters the physical power dynamic – the victim is seated, restricted, trapped by her attackers, unable to defend herself physically from the abuse. It is most horrifying because it is so recognizable: a symbol of the crimes against our humanity that are still being committed, be it to the disabled, the child, the elderly, the poor, the sexual minority, the woman, the outsider, the person of different faith. It revealed the bullying and sadistic power games we recognize all too often in the violence of our world and the way that those who become the scape-goats are often the most vulnerable. When they crucified Christ they lifted Fiona to her feet and pushed the wheelchair over, its wheels spinning. The actor who nailed her to the cross found himself weeping. And Christ stood before us holding and held up by her torturers: holding in her body the sin of the world and saying to us it is here, here in this most painful and broken place that God's transformation begins. Because, strangely, it is not Christ who is vanquished; Fiona showed us that it is the perpetrator who is defeated, for in putting to death Christ they put to death themselves and it is Christ who rises before us. The disciples pushed Fiona away, her crumpled body splayed out in her wheelchair, the life and energy like a spring still visible in her limbs, like the light that can never be extinguished.

Fiona wrote to me:

I'm still humbled and moved to have been a part of it, and grateful to have been offered a frightening but wonderful opportunity to grow in faith and understanding. It was and continues to be a deeply enriching experience. What deeper experience can there be of not only going from the edge to the centre but to become that centre – to actually speak Christ's words and embody his actions – you can't do that without feeling something of what Christ is feeling and what that means for today.

Another year Sam from Afghanistan played the part of Jesus. He had come to the UK as an asylum seeker at the age of 15, arriving alone after a journey across Europe. Seven years ago I met him for the first time. His Farsi translator had brought him to see me. He had come to St Martin's wanting to ask questions about the Christian faith to which he was drawn. He saw in Christianity a kindness and a mercy that attracted him. He was searching for belonging and to make sense of his painful past, the loss of his parents, the violence he had witnessed and been subject to. He spoke of the way as a Christian there 'were no half people' but all were equal – male or female, whoever you were and wherever you had come from. He tested the water of the Christian faith, questioning, not wanting to rush into anything. He went to two confirmation courses before deciding he wanted to be converted and was baptized and confirmed by the Bishop of London. Later, when he reached the age of 21, the Home Office ruled against him on the grounds that they believed his conversion was not genuine. In the Home Office test he had been asked to name the Ten Commandments and he had said, 'You must love the Lord your God with all your heart, and love your neighbour as yourself.' A pretty good summary of the law according to Jesus Christ, but the Home Office marked him wrong, it was not on their answer paper. Then they asked him what the seven deadly sins were and Sam said that he was sorry but he hadn't learnt them yet. At his Appeal hearing there were five witnesses from St Martin's, including three priests, defending his integrity and presenting a letter from the Bishop. He had built relationships of trust with us all and we were there to defend him. The Home Office gave up the fight to deport him and he was given indefinite leave to remain. Yet still it was not an easy journey: a young Afghani trying to navigate the complexities of a foreign culture alone. On top of this he was the victim of an unprovoked attack in which he was hit in the face, and three operations later one of his eyes is still permanently damaged. When I asked him to play the part of Jesus he responded that he never believed that someone like him could ever play the part of Jesus. Yet the story of Christ was written in his life – his journey of redemption, the scars and trauma of his past, the violence done to him, the suffering he had been through, all of this the inextinguishable hope of salvation.

He agreed to play Jesus with a mixture of fear and excitement. I quickly realized it would mean a lot of hard work and practice, but Sam was up for it, coming in at night when the church quietened to run through and practise his lines with his girlfriend via Skype. At first formal, defensive and apologetic, he found it hard to communicate the love and warmth of Jesus for his disciples and the anxiety of his pending betrayal. It was, however, in the scenes of suffering, torture and rejection that Sam began to identify with Christ, and his expression of Christ moved from head to instinct. The disciples were a rag-tag bunch. One, it turned out, was days away from being elected churchwarden, another was a homeless UK national who often attends weekday Morning Prayer. Judas was an Indonesian congregation member whose journey of self-discovery had led him to the USA and then the UK and a civil partnership celebrated among the members of our church. He knew the meaning of betrayal himself, for his own parents, learning of his sexuality, had disowned him. The other nine were members of the weekly 45-strong asylum-seekers group that meets every Sunday afternoon, many of them experiencing homelessness and destitution in London – including a Kurdish Iranian, a Ugandan, a Dominican Republican, a Bangladeshi, a Kenyan, a Zimbabwean and a South African. One is a Ghanaian who spent two years travelling to the UK, crossing the Mediterranean from North Africa in a boat and waiting for many weeks in the Calais Jungle. At the Last Supper they gathered around Jesus, waiting on his every word, knowing from their own lives what it means to hope and pray for salvation.

Those who arrested and tortured Jesus were dressed like the FBI – the epitome of white machismo. And then he faced his accusers in their suits and ties like the politicians of our day, planning, justifying and manipulating a human outrage because it was expedient and necessary for their own power and authority. The guards stripped Jesus of his White Afghan juba and dressed him not in a purple robe but in an orange boiler suit. Instead of whipping this Christ, they waterboarded him. Jesus gasped for air but they pushed him back under, and as they mocked and spat upon him they took selfies with their mobiles. In the congregation everything had gone deathly quiet. 'Weep for your children.' The Passion had taken on a frightening reality, for here, standing before us, were the tortured young of our time and we in sorrow and in shame saw our own lives hung up. A middle-aged American man played Pilate. When he said, 'What is truth?' we in the congregation shivered. When he said, 'The people have spoken', we shivered again. Above the altar this innocent man was nailed to the cross, his agony taken up in the distorted cross of the window through which the refracted light beyond poured in shards. 'My God, my God, why have you forsaken me?' Jesus screamed out from that cross. We were watching the tragedy of our times: the violent murder of the innocent, be it in Syria or Yemen, or Iraq, or Sudan or Afghanistan, or a on a London bridge or outside a mosque in Finsbury. Our homeless disciples came towards him in bewilderment, their arms reaching out towards his body. Slowly and gently they took him down from the cross and laid him on the altar. The Ghanaian who played the Beloved Disciple took his body in his arms with such compassion and care it was clear he'd done such things many times before. The dispossessed disciples gathered around the man they had loved laid out upon the cold stone of the altar, and we were overcome with sorrow for our world and longing for redemption. Then together, very slowly, they lifted his body from the altar and gently laid him to rest behind the altar, backing off as though unable to look away, they closed the sanctuary gates and quietly disappeared leaving two women weeping at the entrance.

A scene from the Passion Drama: Jesus is laid on the altar

Responding to this Passion Drama, Sam Wells wrote:

> The British public sees asylum seekers as a threat or at best an administrative burden. The churches tend to see them as objects of pity and mercy. On Palm Sunday they were none of these things. They were prophets, preachers, provocative witnesses to the gospel, challenging us at St Martin's, used to thinking of ourselves as edgy and politically engaged, with the question of where we each stood in the Passion story. This was the first time our International Group has led us into worship. In the past, members of the group have joined our fellowship by acting as wicketkeeper or demon opening bowler in our cricket team, or as waiter for our hospitality events. But on Palm Sunday they were swept up into the Passion Narrative itself. And they changed the whole way we thought about the story we thought we knew.
>
> Sam from Afghanistan sums up St Martin's because he is the asylum seeker who played Jesus in the drama and was waterboarded for our salvation. He sums up St Martin's because we aren't about condescendingly making welcome alienated strangers, but instead about seeking out the rejected precisely because they are the energy and the life force that will transform us all. Sam sums up our community not because he gratefully received our pity but because he boldly showed us the heart of God.

And I think they were changed themselves too. After the performance I spoke to Sam on the phone. 'How do you feel?' I asked him having played the part of Jesus in front of everyone in the church. 'I feel really amazed by it. It is the best thing I have ever done in my life,' he said. 'I feel there is a lightness in my heart and mind and I understand now why people love Jesus, I feel the same too, closer to him, and for the first time I can be good.'

Passion Drama Script

Narrator 1	On the first day of Unleavened Bread the disciples came to Jesus, saying:
Disciples	Where do you want us to make the preparations for you to eat the Passover?
Narrator 1	Jesus said:
Jesus	Go into the city and you will find a man, and say to him, 'The Teacher says, "My time is near; I will keep the Passover at your house with my disciples."'
Narrator 1	So the disciples did as Jesus had directed them, and they prepared the Passover meal. When it was evening, he took his place with the Twelve; and while they were eating, he said:
Jesus	Truly I tell you, one of you will betray me.
Narrator 1	And they became greatly distressed and began to say to him one after another:
Disciple 1	Surely not I!
Disciple 2	Not I, Lord!
Disciple 1	Surely not I. I will never betray you, Jesus!
Narrator 1	He answered:
Jesus	The one who has dipped his hand into the bowl with me will betray me.
Narrator 1	Judas, who betrayed him, said:
Judas	Surely not I, Rabbi?
Jesus	It is you who have said so.
Narrator 1	While they were eating, Jesus took a loaf of bread, and after blessing it he broke it, gave it to the disciples, and said:
Jesus	Take, eat; this is my body which is given for you. Do this in remembrance of me.
Narrator 1	Then he took a cup, and after giving thanks he gave it to them, saying,
Jesus	Drink this, all of you; for this is my blood which is poured out for many for the forgiveness of sins. Do this as often as you drink it in remembrance of me.

Narrator 1	When they had sung the hymn, they went out to the Mount of Olives. Then Jesus said to them:
Jesus	You will all become deserters because of me this night and run away.
Narrator 1	Peter said to him:
Peter	Though all become deserters because of you, I will never desert you.
Narrator 1	Jesus said to him:
Jesus	Truly I tell you, this very night, before the cock crows, you will deny me three times.
Narrator 1	Peter said to him:
Peter	Even though I must die with you, I will not deny you. I will never deny you, Jesus! Even if the others were to lose their faith and run away it would never be me!
Disciples	We will never deny you, Lord!
Narrator 2	Then Jesus went with them to a place called Gethsemane; and he said to his disciples:
Jesus	Sit here while I go over there and pray.
Narrator 2	He took with him Peter and the two sons of Zebedee, and began to be grieved and agitated. Then he said to them:
Jesus	I am deeply troubled, remain here, and stay awake with me.
Narrator 2	And going a little farther, he threw himself on the ground and prayed,
Jesus	My Father, if it is possible, let this cup pass from me; yet not what I want but what you want.
Narrator 2	Then he came to the disciples and found them sleeping; and he said to Peter:
Jesus	So, could you not stay awake with me one hour? Stay awake and pray.
Narrator 2	Again he went away for the second time and prayed, 'My Father, if this cannot pass unless I drink it, your will be done.' Again he came and found them sleeping, for their eyes were heavy. So leaving them again, he went away and prayed

	for the third time, saying the same words. Then he came to the disciples and said to them:
Jesus	Are you still sleeping and taking your rest? See, the Son of Man is betrayed into the hands of sinners. Look my betrayer is coming.
Narrator 1	While he was still speaking, Judas, one of the Twelve, arrived; with him was a large crowd with swords and clubs, from the chief priests and the elders of the people. Now the betrayer had given them a sign, saying:
Judas	The one I will kiss is the man; arrest him.
Narrator 1	At once he came up to Jesus and said –
Judas	Greetings, Rabbi!
Narrator 1	and kissed him. Jesus said to him:
Jesus	Friend, do quickly what you are here to do.
Narrator 1	Then they came and laid hands on Jesus and arrested him. Suddenly, one of those with Jesus put his hand on his sword, drew it and struck the slave of the high priest, cutting off his ear. Then Jesus said to him:
Jesus	Put your sword back into its place; for all who live by the sword will die by the sword.
Narrator 1	Then all the disciples deserted him and fled. Those who had arrested Jesus took him to Caiaphas the high priest, in whose house the scribes and the elders had gathered.
Narrator 2	But Peter was following him at a distance, as far as the courtyard of the high priest; and going inside, he sat with the guards in order to see how this would end. Now the chief priests and the whole council were looking for false testimony against Jesus so that they might put him to death, but they found none, though many false witnesses came forward. At last two came forward and said:
Witness	This fellow said, 'I am able to destroy the temple of God and to build it in three days.'
Narrator 1	The high priest stood up and said:

High priest 1	Have you no answer? What is it that they testify against you?
High priest 2	Have you no answer to give us?
Narrator 1	But Jesus was silent. Then the high priest said to him:
High priest 1	I put you under oath before the living God, tell us if you are the Messiah, the Son of the living God?
High priest 2	Are you the Messiah, the Son of the living God?
Narrator 1	Jesus said to him:
Jesus	You have said so. But I tell you, From now on you will see the Son-of-Man seated at the right hand of God and coming on the clouds of heaven.
Narrator 1	Then the high priest tore his clothes and said:
High priest 1	Blasphemy!
High priest 2	Blasphemy!
High priest 1	You have heard his blasphemy.
High priest 2	We have heard his blasphemy.
High priest 1	We don't need to call any more witnesses.
High priest 2	Why should we need any more witnesses? We have now all heard his blasphemy. What is your verdict?
Narrator 1	They answered:
High priest 1	GUILTY!
High priest 2	GUILTY!
High priest 1	He deserves death.
High priest 2	Death!
High priest 1	The guilty must die.
High priest 2	The guilty must die.
Narrator 1	Then they spat in his face and struck him; and some slapped him, saying:
High priest 1	Prophesy to us, you Messiah! Who is it that struck you?
High priest 2	Guess who hit you?
Narrator 2	Now Peter was sitting outside in the courtyard. A servant came to him and said,
Servant 1	You also were with Jesus, I know you were, I saw you with him!

Narrator 2	But he denied it before all of them, saying:
Peter	I do not know what you are talking about.
Narrator 2	When he went out to the porch, another servant saw him, and he said to the bystanders:
Servant 2	This man was with Jesus of Nazareth, I know he was.
Narrator 2	Again he denied it with an oath:
Peter	I do not know the man.
Narrator 2	After a little while the bystanders came up and said to Peter:
Servant 3	You are also one of them, I recognize your accent.
Narrator 2	Then he began to curse, and he swore an oath:
Peter	I do not know the man!
Narrator 2	At that moment the cock crowed. Then Peter remembered what Jesus had said: 'Before the cock crows, you will deny me three times.' And he went out and wept bitterly.
Narrator 1	All the chief priests and the elders of the people conferred together against Jesus in order to bring about his death. They bound him, led him away, and handed him over to Pilate the Governor. When Judas, his betrayer, saw that Jesus was condemned, he repented and brought back the 30 pieces of silver to the chief priests and the elders. He said:
Judas	I have sinned by betraying innocent blood.
Narrator 1	But they said:
Chief priest 1	What is that to us? See to it yourself.
Judas	I did not do it for the money or for you.
Chief priest 2	It means nothing to us.
Judas	I did it for him!
Chief priest 1	It means nothing to us. You made your own decision.
Judas	Don't you understand, I did it for him.
Narrator 1	Throwing down the pieces of silver in the temple, he departed; and he went and hanged himself.
Narrator 1	Now Jesus stood before the Governor; and the Governor asked him:

Pilate	Are you the King of the Jews?
Narrator 1	Jesus said:
Jesus	You say so.
Pilate	So you are a king, then.
Jesus	For this I was born and came into the world to testify to the truth. Everyone who belongs to the truth listens to my voice.
Pilate	What is truth?
Narrator 1	Pilate said to the chief priests and elders:
Pilate	I find no case against him.
Pharisee 1	He blasphemes.
Pharisee 2	The people have decided – this man is an enemy of the people.
Pilate	Do you not hear how many accusations they make against you?
Narrator 1	But he gave him no answer, not even to a single charge, so that the Governor was greatly amazed.
Pilate	Do you refuse to speak to me? Do you not know I have the power to release you or the power to have you crucified?
Jesus	You have no power over me unless it has been given to you from above.
Narrator 1	Now at the festival the Governor was accustomed to release a prisoner for the crowd, anyone whom they wanted. At that time they had a notorious prisoner, called Jesus Barabbas. So after they had gathered, Pilate said to them:
Pilate	Whom do you want me to release for you, Jesus Barabbas or Jesus who is called the Messiah?
Narrator 1	For he realized that it was out of jealousy that they had handed him over. While he was sitting on the judgement seat, his wife sent word to him,
Narrator 2	Have nothing to do with that innocent man, for today I have suffered a great deal because of a dream about him.
Narrator 1	Now the chief priests and the elders persuaded the crowds to ask for Barabbas and to have Jesus killed. The Governor again said to them:

Pilate	Which of the two do you want me to release for you?
Narrator 1	And they shouted:
All	**Barabbas.**
Narrator 1	Pilate said to them:
Pilate	Then what should I do with Jesus who is called the Messiah?
Narrator 1	All of them said:
All	**Let him be crucified!**
Pilate	Why, what evil has he done?
Narrator 1	But they shouted all the more:
All	**Let him be crucified!**
Pilate	Do you want me to crucify your king?
All	**We have no king but Caesar! We have no king but Caesar!**
Narrator 1	So when Pilate saw that he could do nothing, but rather that a riot was beginning, he took some water and washed his hands before the crowd, saying:
Pilate	I am innocent of this man's blood; see to it yourselves.
Narrator 1	Then the people as a whole answered:
All	**Let his blood be on us and on our children!**
Narrator 1	So he released Barabbas for them; and after flogging Jesus, he handed him over to be crucified.
Pilate	Release Barabbas and have this Jesus flogged. Take him away and crucify your king. The people have decided!

Music begins: On the willows (Stephen Schwartz) – *(piano only)*

Narrator 2	Then the soldiers of the Governor took Jesus into the Governor's headquarters, and they gathered the whole cohort around him. They stripped him and put a robe on him, and after twisting some thorns into a crown, they put it on his head.

On the willows – verse 1 *(sung)*
Piano continues (improvised)

They put a reed in his right hand and knelt before him and mocked him, saying:

All **Hail, King of the Jews!**

Narrator 1 They spat on him, and took the reed and struck him on the head. After mocking him, they stripped him of the robe. Then they led him away to crucify him.

On the willows – verse 2 *(sung)*

Narrator 2 And when they came to a place called Golgotha (which means Place of a Skull), they offered him wine to drink, mixed with gall; but when he tasted it, he would not drink it. And they crucified him, they divided his clothes among themselves by casting lots; then they sat down there and kept watch over him. Over his head they put the charge against him, which read:

All **'This is Jesus, the King of the Jews.'**

Narrator 2 Then two bandits were crucified with him, one on his right and one on his left. Those who passed by derided him, shaking their heads and saying:

Chief priest 1 You who would destroy the temple and build it in three days, save yourself! If you are the Son of God, come down from the cross.

Narrator 2 In the same way the chief priests also, along with the scribes and elders, were mocking him, saying:

Chief priest 2 He saved others; he cannot save himself. He is the King of Israel; let him come down from the cross now, and we will believe in him.

Chief priest 1 He trusts in God; let God deliver him now, if he wants to; for he said, 'I am God's Son.'

Narrator 2 The bandits who were crucified with him also taunted him in the same way.

Narrator 1	Then Jesus said:
Jesus	Father, forgive them, they do not know what they are doing!

Benedictus *(Karl Jenkins) (accompaniment/ introduction only)*

Narrator 2	From noon on, darkness came over the whole land until three in the afternoon. And about three o'clock Jesus cried with a loud voice:
Jesus	Eli, Eli, lema sabachthani? My God, my God, why have you forsaken me?
Narrator 2	When some of the bystanders heard it, they said, 'This man is calling for Elijah.'
High priest 1	Wait, let us see whether Elijah will come to save him.
Narrator 2	Then Jesus cried again with a loud voice:
Jesus	Father, into your hands I give my Spirit. It is finished.
Narrator 2	And Jesus breathed his last.
Narrator 1	At that moment the curtain of the temple was torn in two, from top to bottom. The earth shook and the rocks were split. The tombs also were opened, and many bodies of the saints who had fallen asleep were raised. Now, when the centurion and those with him, who were keeping watch over Jesus, saw the earthquake and what took place, they were terrified and said:
Andrew	Truly this man was God's Son!

Benedictus *(continues sung as disciples take the body of Jesus down from the cross and lay him in the grave)*

Narrator 1	The women who had followed Jesus from Galilee stood at a distance watching these things. When it was evening, there came a rich man from Arimathea, named Joseph, who was also a disciple of Jesus. He went to Pilate and asked

for the body of Jesus; then Pilate ordered it to be given to him. So Joseph took the body and wrapped it in a clean linen cloth and laid it in his own new tomb, which he had hewn in the rock. He then rolled a great stone to the door of the tomb and went away. It was the day of preparation and the Sabbath was beginning. The women who had come with him from Galilee followed and they saw the tomb and how his body was laid. Then they returned and prepared spices and ointments. On the Sabbath they rested according to the commandment.

Silence

Choir   I know that my redeemer lives (Richard Jeffrey-Gray) *(sung by the choir)*

St Luke's Day

Fiona MacMillan

Like many churches, St Martin's marks St Luke's Day by offering prayers for healing at the main Sunday Eucharist. In 2012, when looking to schedule a new conference on disability and church, the feast day of Luke the physician seemed both a good enough hook and a reasonably quiet time in the diary. Over the last five years this particular timing has played an important part in our community's growing understanding of disability and of healing.

Historically the Church has often been found caring for people on the edge of society. For hundreds of years the Church challenged, led and changed the wider culture through its valuing of those who are powerless. It practised faith in action by feeding, housing and caring for people who otherwise would have suffered or died through poverty or sickness. Many great institutions, hospitals and charities have their origins in people living out their faith, particularly in the nineteenth century.

But since the 1960s the disability rights movement has campaigned for greater autonomy, and the Church has been slower than society to respond to what is a significant sector of the population. In the UK today there are around 11 million people living with a disabling physical, sensory, cognitive or mental health condition, of whom 80 per cent were born healthy and have had to learn to adjust. All of us spend our lives somewhere on a spectrum between the super-fit athlete and the profoundly impaired person, moving and changing as a result of accident, illness or ageing. Disabled people may be an uncomfortable presence in a society lauding strength, but in the Church, which professes a paradox of vulnerability, we're often objects for pastoral attention rather than agents of change.

The Church of the twenty-first century frequently fails disabled people, hearing echoes of an understanding that links sickness with sinfulness, mental health issues with possession, and disability as being in need of cure. Pounced on by street evangelists, spoken about rather than listened to, regarded as difficult or demanding, costly or time-consuming, it's not surprising that many disabled people are put off going to church – even if we can get in. Access is often focused on getting in – ramps and lifts, hearing loops and loos – rather than joining in, with participation seen as a step too far. We are more likely to be known by our needs than celebrated for our gifts.

St Martin's began to explore the experience of disability in 2011, as part of our commitment to working with those often excluded from church. Disabled people face significant barriers to access and participation and are particularly vulnerable to the impact of austerity cuts in wider society and the Church. Our focus is twofold: working within our own community, and sharing our resources and learning more widely. Both are centred on the experience and ideas of disabled people. Within St Martin's we're led by the Disability Advisory Group, which brings together people with experience of physical, sensory, cognitive or mental health conditions, either from our own lives or from living alongside others in our caring or work role. Open meetings once a term explore issues and ideas – both barriers to belonging and the insights that grow from living vulnerably –

and share our learning and resources with the congregation and community in a variety of ways.

More widely, we work in partnership with Inclusive Church to hold an annual conference on disability and church. Centred on lived experience, underpinned by theology and modelling belonging, it is planned by and for disabled people to resource each other and the Church. Over the past five years we've drawn more than 300 delegates from across the country to explore gifts and share ideas of presence, paradox and prophetic ministry.

Thus in October 2012, on the Saturday before St Luke's Day, we found ourselves part of a gathered community of disabled people exploring disability and church. There were people with wheelchairs, sticks, or support dogs, hearing aids or hidden conditions; friends and supporters, with a healthy sprinkling of interested professionals. It was an exciting and energizing embodiment of the Kingdom and we were inspired. The following day we joined the Sunday morning service and listened to lessons, sang hymns and heard anthems, which all used the language of sickness and sin, blindness as lack of insight and choruses of the leaping lame – a rude return to reality.

Developing this service has been an integral part of our learning, as individuals, groups and the whole community explore ideas of disability and healing. The second year was a leap forward, with a special liturgy written by our lecturer in inclusive theology, members of the Disability Advisory Group (DAG) reading lessons, leading intercessions and assisting with the distribution of communion. The preacher was the keynote speaker from the conference the day before. It was good to be sharing our ideas and made for a visible presence, but we weren't yet using the gifts and gathered wisdom we'd been given.

In 2014 the DAG had spent some time exploring biblical healing stories, reimagining them from our perspectives as un-cured disabled people. In early summer a small group met to review the St Luke's Day service, deciding which parts of the service were necessary and which could be changed. We chose readings, one from the lectionary and another that brought in a helpful theme. We set aside an hour of the regular DAG meeting for a liturgy-writing workshop; Sam agreed to lead this and to write a worksheet. About a dozen people worked in twos and threes to write a confession, intercessions, fraction, invitation and thanksgiving. These were sent in to be polished and put together, and in early September the small group met again to review, choose some music and think through people and logistics. The result was a service where anyone could lead, read or preach, while the DAG's ideas were woven into the fabric of the liturgy itself.

Over the last couple of years the service has continued to develop. We were inspired to invite the healing team to join the DAG in a stand-alone workshop, sharing our learning about disability and healing as we wrote parts of the liturgy together. The liturgy gives us an opportunity to share more widely something that connects faithfully from our experience, using the gifts of living vulnerably.

Sometimes the service brings an opportunity for usually not very visible people to become more visible; participation that might not work on a regular basis can become symbolic as we model something of the gathered company of saints. One year a DAG member with Alzheimer's was invited to assist with the distribution of communion. Her vociferous lifelong campaigning for women's equality, including women's ordination, had sometimes been distorted by deep disappointment and anger. Here, at the heart of the service, assisted by a faithful friend, she held the ciborium and gazed at each person approaching with a luminous and loving intensity – weakness transformed into intense presence.

The St Luke's Day service has become an important part of what's now a weekend of activities. We share insights and ideas within the wider congregation, while conference delegates get to stay on and experience something of regular St Martin's. Some are coming to church for the first time in many years. The liturgy has shaped the weekend, reflecting the place we're in and being shaped by the people who come.

How to – what's good to know/do

- Have lived experience at the heart, weaving it in rather than adding it on. Engage, explain, involve. (What is healing? What is disability?) Explore the idea with one or two people, do some initial thinking/planning of the service. If it seems too much, what's a good start?
- Workshop – directly invite people/groups with lived experience and advertise more widely. Many people don't identify as 'disabled' but as 'only' living with an illness/condition/impairment. Open meetings encourage wider participation. If people are struggling, ask for response in single words or short phrases to describe their experience or feelings, and weave their words into the liturgy.
- Words matter. Language that uses blindness as wilful avoidance or deaf as refusing to hear may not make for a good welcome. Edit or explain things that are unhelpful. Choose hymns carefully, adapt as appropriate. Helpful hymns include 'We cannot measure how you heal' (John Bell), 'O Christ the Healer, we have come' (Fred Pratt Green), 'O God, you search me and you know me' (Bernadette Farrell).
- There's a dearth of anthems specifically for St Luke's Day as most use unhelpful texts, but plenty that focus on universal need for wholeness, weakness/strength etc.
- We expect larger than usual numbers of people with additional needs – whether coming with wheelchairs, walking aids or support dogs, needing to sit where a hearing loop works well or to get up and walk around during the service. Make sure stewards have got good knowledge and understanding of what facilities are available and how they work. It's really helpful to give information and invite people to ask for what they need. Don't worry about not knowing everything – a friendly welcome is by far the most important thing.
- People go straight from communion to healing rather than back to their places and out again. We've brought distribution of communion forward from the altar to the front of the chancel, as well as our usual distribution at the top of side aisles. The healing team are at three points in front of the altar rail,

which gives universal access to step-free healing. It might also be helpful to have one position with a chair for those who find it difficult to stand. The choir goes up into the organ loft so that the healing is more private – and more audible.

- We're learning as we go, as much as by the things that don't work well as those that do. Looking around the table – who's not here? Are we modelling belonging? This year we'll have BSL for the first time, which feels exciting.

Liturgy-writing workshop – worksheet

Confession
- Invitation: addressed to the congregation, recalling God's purpose, our messing that purpose, and God's mercy in longing to restore us.
- Three kyries, addressed to God, Trinitarian perhaps, balanced, direct, not preachy.
- Work in themes from readings.

Intercessions

- Four petitions.
- Fivefold structure:
  - Address (e.g. 'Disabled God')
  - Narrative ('who in your crucified son Jesus could not move your hands or feet')
  - Petition ('visit your children who live with disadvantage, pain, hardship and fear')
  - Desired outcome ('that they may see you face to face and be renewed in your service')
  - Sign-off ('Lord in your mercy').
- Work in themes from readings.

Eucharistic Prayer

- First section – three sentences, covering creation, Israel, coming of Christ, leading into joining with angels.
- Start of second section – two sentences, one connecting Christ to Last Supper/communion, one invoking Spirit on congregation and on bread and wine.
- (Second part of second section does not change – words of institution.)
- Third section, intercession and doxology – three sentences turning themes from readings into intercession for church, unity, justice, emerging into expectation of final fulfilment.

Fraction and Invitation

- Words to mark breaking of the bread – with or without congregational response.
- Words to invite people to the altar, with or without congregational response.

Post-Communion Prayer

- To include thanksgiving for communion.
- Also to include thanksgiving for other things.

Sample service

We set out our understanding of disability and healing in a note inside the cover of the service booklet:

St Martin-in-the-Fields is an inclusive church and we try to up-hold a broad understanding of inclusion. An important part of this, reflected in the St Martin's Action Plan, is to increase our understanding of disability so that our welcome can be open to all. We still have a way to go, and are grateful to our Disability Advisory Group who are leading and encouraging us in this aim. Members of the group and of the healing team have together contributed to the liturgy for this service, where we celebrate St Luke and his witness to a healing that embraces wholeness, compassion and justice.

Welcome

Poem written and read by member of the Disability Advisory Group

Greeting

Opening Hymn

Confession

Let us confess our sins to God the wounded healer, who turns our places of pain into altars of hope and our sins into moments of renewal.

Amid your abundance, we fear we are not enough; amid your acceptance, we judge others for failing to live up to our image of them; amid your inclusion, we label and condemn. Lord, have mercy.
Lord, have mercy.

Despite your generosity, we fail to forgive others and do not allow ourselves to be forgiven; despite your grace, we hold fast to our image of ourselves; despite your healing and new life, we prefer to hold on to the difficulty and dreariness of what we know. Lord, have mercy.
Lord, have mercy

For all your incarnate presence, we fail to see we are created in your image, unique and precious in your sight; for all your mercy, we are quick to blame and slow to understand; for all your resurrection, we hold onto the pain of the past as a weapon in the present and a shield against the future. Lord, have mercy.
Lord, have mercy.

Absolution

Gloria

Collect

Reading

Gospel hymn

Gospel

Sermon

Intercessions

Peace

Offertory Hymn

Offertory Response
God of blessing,
we bring you these gifts.
Broken God,
make us whole.

Eucharistic Prayer
Creator God, we thank and praise you, for by your Holy Spirit you parted the waters in creation and in the paths of liberation you journey with us through deep and shallow waters. On the great night of Passover your children ate the bread of affliction, unleavened and unfinished, before they journeyed into the desert. In your Son Jesus, our friend and brother, you journeyed from heaven to earth, and from life to death to life again. So your journeying people now join with all the company of heaven and all on earth to sing your thanks and praise.

When your Son Jesus Christ met with his disciples on the night before he died, they recalled how, once before, the bread of affliction had become the bread of hope. Send down your Holy Spirit upon your Church, that in its affliction of body, mind or spirit it may discover in you the God of hope. Sanctify this bread and cup, that they may be for us the body and blood

of our Lord Jesus Christ; who, at supper with his disciples ...
[words of institution]

Broken yet healing God, gather us together from many dwelling places to feast together at one table. Through this meal unite us with Jesus, with one another, and with the whole of creation. Make your church, nourished by this bread and wine, a place of common voice with room for all. Embolden your people to step out into the waters too deep for human understanding, that they may spread their nets with the whole of creation. Wounded as you are, show us again how to walk a rising road. Bring together the fresh water of healing and the salt water of justice in your Kingdom, prepared for us through Jesus the way, the truth and the life. Hasten the day when all hopes are fulfilled, all fears erased and all pain assuaged in the fullness of your Son and the power of your Spirit, holy Father. **Amen.**

Fraction and Invitation
We break this bread
In memory of Christ, broken for us.
Come to this table just as you are. Come to meet the incarnate, broken Jesus. Come, bring your strengths for healing and your brokenness in celebration. Come, for it is Christ who invites you as you are.

Distribution and Prayers for Healing
We offer this invitation and guidance:
You are invited, after receiving communion, if you so wish, to come forward to the altar rail for prayer for healing, anointing and the laying on of hands. Please line up behind the choir stalls and go to a station when it becomes available. One of those offering prayer will ask if there is something or someone you wish to pray for in particular, and you are welcome to say a few words to give some context. The person will then say a prayer on your behalf as they lay a hand on your shoulder or head, and they will anoint you with oil on your forehead. You may then return to your seat.

Communion hymn /Anthems/Music during distribution and healing

Thanksgiving

> Gentle and gracious God, we thank you for situations you create where people can flourish, and the space you make where we can heal each other. We humbly praise you that you have so wonderfully created us and made a place for each one of us. We treasure before you the gift of healing, of new life, and of a Kingdom in which the weak are strong and the strong are weak. You make all things new, meet us in our brokenness and begin again with us today; through Jesus Christ our Lord. Amen

Notices

Blessing

Hymn

Dismissal

Patronal Festival

Samuel Wells

Each year on the weekend nearest 11 November, St Martin's Day, the different parts of St Martin-in-the-Fields – the congregation, the commercial enterprise, The Connection (the homeless centre) the Charity (based around the BBC Radio 4 Christmas Appeal), the Trust (which is the principal fundraising instrument), and the Chinese congregation – come together to reaffirm and celebrate our common purpose. There are several challenges: the service is in English (not Chinese), it is on the congregation's territory, not all involved are Christians, not everyone understands the detailed nature of one another's work and commitments. And yet it is invariably a vibrant occasion. Finishing with a shared meal and a ceilidh often helps.

The secret is to identify some aspect of our common life that everyone appreciates but no one speaks about to any great extent. One year we focused on the notion of a living mystery. The philosopher Gabriel Marcel talks about a problem and a mystery. A problem is something generic that you see replicated frequently and you learn technical skills to be able to fix. You can walk round the outside of it. A mystery is something you enter. You can only appreciate it from the inside. You've never encountered it before. It can't be fixed – it can only be appreciated, enjoyed, to some extent understood.

> A problem is something which I meet, which I find completely before me, but which I can therefore lay siege to and reduce. But a mystery is something in which I am myself involved, and it can therefore only be thought of as a sphere where the distinction between what is in me and what is before me loses its meaning and initial validity.[7] ... When I am dealing with a problem, I am trying to discover a solution that can become common property, that consequently can, at least in theory, be rediscovered by anybody at all. But ... this idea of a validity for 'anybody at all' or of a thinking in general has less and less application the more deeply one penetrates into the inner courts of philosophy.[8]

When I lived in America it used to really annoy me when people said 'Washington is broken' or 'Our public school system is broken', because it suggested these things were machines that just needed a technician to fix. It comes from a mindset that's captivated by the language of problem and solution. But most things, and certainly most people, that are troubled can't simply be fixed. Instead they can be heard, encouraged, challenged, healed, forgiven, reconciled.

The Jesus we see at the Transfiguration isn't a solution to a problem, whether that problem be death or sin or evil. He's an invitation to enter a mystery. Moses and Elijah have clearly

---

7 Gabriel Marcel, *Being and Having*, trans. Katharine Farrer, London: Dacre Press, 1949, p. 117.

8 Gabriel Marcel, *The Mystery of Being*, vol. 1, *Reflection and Mystery*, trans. G. S. Fraser, London: The Harvill Press, 1950, p. 213.

entered that mystery in a big way: the disciples are being invited too. Peter clumsily offers to build a bit of real estate to accommodate Jesus' companions. He's trying to fix a problem. But Jesus isn't fixing a problem. He's saying come and join me in the heart of the mystery.

In the service outlined below, we heard five brief but heartfelt and extraordinary testimonies of life at St Martin-in-the-Fields. With all our busyness and activity and the numbers of people who throng our buildings you'd think we were a remarkably effective solution to people's problems. But we're not. We're not a solution to anything. Cardinal Suhard, who was the leader of the Catholic Church in France in the 1940s, said the famous words, 'To be a witness does not consist in engaging in propaganda, nor even in stirring people up, but in being a living mystery. It means to live in such a way that one's life would not make sense if God did not exist.'

Every part of St Martin-in-the-Fields is a living mystery. It's a vision of a ladder of angels, pitched, in Francis Thompson's famous words, 'betwixt heaven and Charing Cross'. It's not that part is worldly, part spiritual, or that part is charitable, part profiteering, or that part is professional, part voluntary, or that part is popular, part aspirational: those are all false distinctions. Right now we're trying to find appropriate ways to help other organizations make the kind of journey we've made; but what we can't do is offer them techniques for fixing their problems – we can only offer them inspiration and support for entering deeper into their mystery.

We'd all like to be proficient at fixing problems. You get such a buzz from being a solution-provider. But the truth is, the most important things in life, like beauty, truth and goodness, like death, poverty, despair and doubt, like desire, companionship, vision, teamwork and love, don't run on a problem–solution framework. And those are the things St Martin's is most deeply about.

St Martin's invites people to visit and/or stay, as a worshipper, client, volunteer, staff member, audience attendee, customer, donor, performer, disciple. The bad news is it's a community that won't fix your problems. The good news is that it's a community of transfiguration – a living mystery.

Service outline

Hymn

Introduction and Opening Prayer

Reading: A Problem and a Mystery (Gabriel Marcel)

Anthem: I thank you, God (Eric Whitacre)

Testimonies

- The congregation as a living mystery
- The Connection as a living mystery
- Choral music as a living mystery

Children's Voices: We are young

Testimonies

- Commercial life as a living mystery
- The Chinese congregation as a living mystery

Hymn

Reading: Luke 9.28–36 – Jesus' Transfiguration

Anthem

Sermon

Anthem

Prayers

Offertory hymn

Blessing

Voluntary

4

On the Edge of the World: Broadcasting

Introduction

St Martin-in-the-Fields is widely known for its architecture, location, royal foundation, classical music and longstanding engagement with homelessness and social vulnerability; but what really made it famous was broadcasting. It hosted the first ever religious broadcast in 1924, began the great tradition of the BBC Radio 4 Christmas Appeal in 1926, and in 1951 Sunday evening broadcast worship from St Martin's had an audience as large as a third of the population. This was what made it the nation's parish church, and, through the World Service, gave it such a high profile around the Empire and later Commonwealth.

Today St Martin's engages with live media in a number of ways. The relationship with the BBC is still crucial and flourishing. Broadcasts of *Sunday Worship* and *Daily Service* on Radio 4 are regular, and the annual Ascension Day live broadcast is always a highlight. Spoken-word contributions to the *Today* programme's 'Thought for the Day' and other such items are also frequent. But the rise of social media and digital communication has brought with it expertise and opportunity that is full of promise. In this chapter we explore how we have tried to capitalize on these opportunities.

Broadcasting

Samuel Wells and Andrew Earis

Any UK citizen who lives for an extended period in another country quickly comes to appreciate the true value of the BBC. Constantly under attack from rivals in the marketplace of broadcasting who resent its privileged status and from political antagonists who are extraordinarily quick to perceive or imagine left-wing bias, the BBC's reputation and reach are incomparable. The fact that its charter requires it to include religious output makes it a unique partner for the church, and the relationship between St Martin-in-the-Fields and the BBC is an integral part of the St Martin's story.

When it comes to worship, St Martin's offers five kinds of services to the BBC.

- There is the annual Ascension Day service, broadcast on Radio 4 from 8 to 9 p.m. on the sixth Thursday after Easter.
- There are frequent live broadcasts, planned two to three months in advance, carefully prepared and rehearsed, usually for *Sunday Worship*, 8.10–8.48 a.m. around three times a year.
- There have been significant occasions of crisis or tragedy when a service at St Martin's has been hastily arranged and prepared after a major event, such as the death of Nelson Mandela or the Nice terrorist attack. Here relationships of trust and a wide range of broadcasting experience make for a rewarding challenge and a responsibility of privilege to express the nation's lament and offer words of faith at a critical moment.
- There are regular pre-recorded *Daily Service* broadcasts, roughly monthly.
- There have been occasional live TV broadcasts, such as the VJ Day Seventieth Anniversary in 2015, and pre-recorded *Songs of Praise* programmes.

To be invited to speak to an enormous audience, often in the millions, is a tremendous privilege. It needs always to be treated as a gesture of trust and regarded with the greatest of respect. The idea that just because the service takes place from your building with mostly your own familiar participants can give the mistaken impression that it is 'your' service. This is misguided; the BBC knows its audience, knows what works, what produces the desired outcome, what can be communicated through this medium, at this time of day, within this time frame. If a sermon is judged to take a wrong tack, a hymn considered unsuitable, a lesson reader inaudible, a reading inappropriate, this is not unjustified interference – it is the guiding hand of experience saving the unwary from embarrassment, offence or humiliation. After a broadcast we invariably receive messages from correspondents who believe we should have 'used' the opportunity of a live microphone to visit upon the listeners a dogmatic message conveying a particular understanding of salvation. Such a perspective represents a misunderstanding of the nature of broadcasting and an inability to grasp what it means to speak generously and respectfully to an immensely diverse audience including devout believers, people on the fringes of faith, agnostics, atheists and people of other faiths.

The principles that have emerged in our pattern of broadcasts include the following:

- Try to offer a diversity of music that engages our choral tradition but includes contemporary evangelical and Catholic renewal elements.
- Affirm people's religious and life experience by inviting three-minute testimonies from those at the sharp end of issues – sometimes from unexpected angles.
- Don't get predictable in subject matter – be playful and challenging in taking up issues (e.g. wishing to but finding oneself unable to bear children) that don't often get a hearing.
- Concentrate on addressing interesting and appropriate subjects in thoughtful ways rather than getting too preachy and criticizing government or society.
- Celebrating without self-congratulation. Adopt a tone of 'We're discovering that …' rather than 'We have a wonderful tradition of …'.

- Modelling forms of prayer (e.g. lament or intercession) can be among the most important things we do.
- A simple gesture, like reading the Lord's Prayer in a foreign language, can do immense good.
- Use the whole Bible, not just familiar passages from the Gospels.
- Make sure the sermon is about God. It seems obvious but it needs saying.

Service outline: A Lament for Nice (prepared at 48 hours' notice for Radio 4's *Sunday Worship*), 17 July 2016

Introit: Lord's Prayer (*Notre Père*) (Maurice Duruflé)

Introduction and Opening Prayer

Hymn: 'O God of all salvation' (Ally Barrett, sung to the tune *King's Lynn*)

Lament

O Lord, how long? How long will we hear of those celebrating a national day being ruthlessly slaughtered? How long will your children dancing and relaxing be blown to high heaven? How long will Baghdad be a byword for mutilation and hatred? How long will those in a concert hall be powerless victims of murder and cruelty?

Do you not listen? Do you not see our sufferings? Do you not bleed with our blood, cry with our tears, hurt with our pain?

We know you will one day bring justice like a never-failing stream; we believe you will at the last vindicate the oppressed; we trust that you will at the end of time raise the downtrodden from the dust. But why will you not do it now? We need it today, Lord. People are howling in anguish that you may meet them in their sorrow and lift their hearts to a new dawn.

What is happening with these extremists? What possesses them to disgrace their own religion and break the hearts of so many people? Can you not bring them face to face with your mercy and compassion and turn their hearts to the ways of gentleness and the paths of peace?

We are tired, we are weak, we are worn; precious Lord, take our hand, lead us on, help us stand.

Bless the peacemakers. Bless the ones who forgive the unforgivable. Bless the ones who refuse to return hatred for hatred. Bless us, Lord, who long for your peace. Gracious God, hear these prayers of your children.

Anthem: Kyrie from Requiem (Maurice Duruflé)

Link

Remarks from the French Ambassador in London

Psalm 55

Reading: Matthew 11.7b–14

Hymn: 'Lead, kindly Light' (J. H. Newman)

Sermon

Anthem: Cantique de Jean Racine (Gabriel Fauré)

Prayers

God of mercy, your Son Jesus wept tears like great drops of blood. Bring comfort to the people of Nice today. Where they are bereaved, send them your grace; where they are injured or in terrible pain, give them companions, doctors, healing; where they are in despair or terror, offer them life, light, time, peace. Bless the French nation; make it one people, with one heart, one soul, one body, one trust, one hope.

God of compassion, your Son wept at the graveside of Lazarus, whom he loved. Lead us in the paths of peace. Visit the people of Orlando, Paris, Baghdad, Istanbul, Birstall, Brussels. Bring vision to this country, to its new Prime Minister and Cabinet, to the opposition and those who debate its leadership. Direct the hearts of all who are confused or angry about how things are and where they are going; show us how to make this country a blessing to all the nations of the world.

God of endless love, your Son's disciples wept at his graveside, and yet beheld his risen glory. Receive those whom we name before you in our hearts, who need your help, your wholeness, your healing hand. In all the crises of your world, show us where we each are called to respond, to reach out, to relate, to restore. Make this time of trial a new beginning in your people's understanding of your ways and your calling. And show us what peace means when violence is so near.

Lord's Prayer (in French)

Hymn: 'Be still, my soul; the Lord is on thy side'

Blessing

Anthem: In paradisum (Gabriel Fauré)

Voluntary

Webcasting

Katherine Hedderly

St Martin's was invited to take part in the Church of England's year-long initiative *Church Live* in 2015/16, broadcasting services live via the social media platform Twitter to global audiences simply through the use of smartphones. *Church Live* provided an opportunity for those unfamiliar with Church of England services to experience worship, prayer and preaching, and 50 churches were involved with the full range of worship styles and church traditions represented from around the country. We live streamed our Advent Parish Eucharist and Advent Carol Service to a global audience of 3,000-plus who joined our congregations with us in church. We had a small dedicated social media team made up of members of the congregation, and, with minimal equipment, a good sound connection and people ready to engage online throughout the service with those joining us from around the world, we were able to welcome many new people to experience worship with us, not just as an audience but with an authentic experience of participation in worship. Questions were answered, explanations of the service were given, prayers received and incorporated into our worship, and our *Church Live* congregation were welcomed with a piece to camera by the worship leader at the beginning of the service and involved throughout the service, included in the prayers and blessed at the end. We helped our live-stream participants to engage with all aspects of our worship and encouraged them to continue to engage with our broadcasts and online resources and follow us as they explored more about the Christian faith, but also to make contact with their local church if they wanted to join a local worshipping community.

There was real opportunity for online ministry and we could see the potential for the mission opportunities this broadcasting could give us, reaching out to participants from across the globe. Following the service we also live streamed the launch of our Annual St Martin's Christmas Appeal, giving viewers a glimpse into the wider life of the St Martin's community and our ministry of care for vulnerable and homeless people.

This Advent Sunday *Church Live* experience encouraged us to explore our own live streaming at Pentecost, using a different social media platform, this time Facebook Live. Again we had a really encouraging response with 2,000-plus engagements on Twitter and Facebook and an 85 per cent engagement rate from those who follow us, showing that there is a real appetite for live broadcasting from the people who follow us.

We subsequently provided a simple 'how to' guide for a number of other churches interested in live streaming but not sure where to start (see below).

These initial steps have laid the foundations for the live-streaming aspect of our global web ministry which we are now taking forward with regular live streaming through the year. Engaging with real-time social media opportunities is an opportunity to proclaim the gospel afresh and reach out in exciting ways.

'How to' guide

- Create a small social media team of digital enthusiasts or experts from the congregation.
- Prepare a communications plan to think about how you make the most of the broadcast. Promoting the event on Facebook with a small ad spend in the week leading up to the service really helped. We targeted influential accounts and asked people to retweet, like or share the messages we posted.
- Engage with your congregation (through the parish bulletin, emails, etc.) to ensure that the live streaming of services is linked into your mission and ministry planning; encourage them to share on social media and in their networks.
- Prepare tweets in advance to use before, during and after the broadcast, which will include details about your church, the service and liturgy, the Christian faith, a link to your website, details of your next broadcast and how people can make contact with their local church.
- Use a modern smartphone with a good camera built in (iPhone 6 or above recommended).
- Have a good internet connection in church. It can be wired or wireless.
- Test all equipment and the connection in advance.
- Use a tripod suitable for smartphone – they are available for between £20 and £30 online.
- Link into the churches' sound system with a sufficiently long sound cable to allow a variety of positions around church. (Most of the issues other churches had with their broadcast was with sound.)
- Have a dedicated team ready to respond live to those joining from around the world who are confident about sharing their faith, the life of the church and responding to people's questions.
- Provide an area in church where those who do not wish to be filmed can sit, and clearly label this area. Make sure you advertise this ahead of the service.

Podcasting

Samuel Wells and Andrew Earis

While webcasting does a great job of making people not present feel they are part of a live event and gives those considering attending a church an excellent sense of what it might be like to worship there, podcasting is a deceptively similar but in practice very different way to reach a wider public than we may ever hope or imagine will ever attend events or services at St Martin's.

A podcast is like a radio programme, but it exists as an audio file. Listeners engage with them not by waiting to tune in at a broadcast time, but by playing them whenever they choose. The reality is that almost everyone has a mobile phone and many people use their phone to listen to live broadcasts or recorded podcasts, not just from established media channels but from anyone with the quality of material worth listening to and the ability to produce that material to a high enough standard.

At St Martin's we use podcasts in three kinds of ways:

1 Recordings of once-live events (e.g. sermons, lectures, interviews). These can be effective but are often much less satisfying than the original experience of actually being there.
2 Repackaged versions of once-live events, re-recorded and heavily edited into a format more suitable for listening via a phone or computer.
3 Specially created small packages that have never had a live airing but are specifically intended for people to receive as a kind of virtual education or worship.

Among the second kind we have produced a number of Great Sacred Music podcasts. In these we take away the introductory and closing remarks (thus not pretending it's a live event) and the hymns (which are there largely to make the audience/congregation feel part of things and ensure it doesn't feel like a regular concert). Instead we create something much more like a bespoke radio broadcast limited to 20 minutes. An example is outlined below.

Among the third kind we have had great success with a weekly Monday morning 8.30 a.m. email that goes to a wide distribution list called Sacred Moments. Like a bite-sized Great Sacred Music, it includes a one-minute spoken introduction connecting a devotional theme to a well-loved hymn, and a three-minute rendition of the hymn recorded at St Martin's. It makes an excellent start to the week but also introduces a wider listenership to a glimpse of what St Martin's can offer them as a community of faith and arts.

Soundcloud is a free service that can be used to share podcasts you produce. Users can subscribe to receive alerts and it integrates with iTunes and other services to help your content reach the widest possible audience. Find out more at www.soundcloud.com.

Outline: Great Sacred Music Podcast – Mrs C. F. Alexander

'Christ be with me'

Cecil Frances Humphreys was born in Dublin in 1818. As a young adult member of the Church of Ireland she came under the influence of the Oxford Movement, and especially John Keble, who fostered in her an Anglo-Catholic sacramental spirituality. In 1848 at the age of 30 she published *Hymns for Little Children*, which went through no fewer than 69 editions before the end of the century. It contained what were to become some of her most famous and enduring hymns, including 'All things bright and beautiful', 'There is a green hill far away' and 'Once in royal David's city'. She used the profits from her celebrated hymnbook to support the Derry and Raphoe Diocesan Institution for the Deaf and Dumb in Strabane. She was also involved with the Derry Home for Fallen Women, and worked to develop a district nurse service. Let's now listen to her hymn about the calling of the first disciples, Jesus calls us o'er the tumult.

'Jesus calls us o'er the tumult'

Cecil Frances caused consternation in her family by taking up with and marrying William Alexander, a Church of Ireland clergyman and poet, who was six years her junior. Hence the name by which she is better known, Mrs C. F. Alexander. William went on to become Bishop of Derry and Archbishop of Armagh in 1867, only adding to his wife's fame. Her carol 'Once in royal David's city' has become known for the treble solo that traditionally opens the King's College, Cambridge, Nine Lessons and Carols. It began as an attempt to explain the Apostles' Creed to a child. The first article of the creed became 'All things bright and beautiful'; the second article, 'who was conceived by the Holy Spirit, / born of the Virgin Mary', became 'Once in royal'. It locates the incarnation between creation and the second coming of Christ, and draws somewhat dated moral conclusions from Jesus' obedient childhood.

'Once in royal' (arr. Will Todd)

The eternal gates lift up their heads continues Cecil Frances' exposition of the Apostles' Creed by describing the ascension of Jesus to heaven. It does so by adopting the language of the twenty-fourth psalm, about letting the king of glory through the eternal gates, and regarding Jesus' ascension as fulfilling this prophecy. Always quick to draw an application, the hymn then asks us to open the gates of our hearts and minds and let the risen Jesus dwell in us as fully as he does in heaven.

'The eternal gates lift up their heads'

The idea for a series of hymns on the Apostles' Creed came from Cecil Frances' godsons, who complained that the catechism, which they were swotting up for confirmation, was difficult and boring. So she wrote a set of verses illustrating the different clauses of the creed for their benefit. Today we love 'the purple-headed mountain'. But the original also contained the more controversial verse, 'The rich man in his castle, the poor man at his gate, God made them high and lowly, And ordered their estate', again illustrating how tied the author was to the social expectations of her era.

'All things bright and beautiful' (John Rutter)

We opened with a part of Cecil Frances' well-known translation of St Patrick's Breastplate, words probably written in the eighth century but attributed to St Patrick during his work in Ireland in the fifth century. H. H. Dickinson, Dean of the Chapel Royal at Dublin Castle, says:

> I wrote to [Cecil Frances] suggesting that she should fill a gap in our Irish Church Hymnal by giving us a metrical version of St. Patrick's 'Lorica' [or breastplate] and I sent her a carefully collated copy of the best prose translations of it. Within a week she sent me that exquisitely beautiful as well as faithful version which appears in the appendix to our Church Hymnal.

The translation was set to music by C. V. Stanford.

'I bind unto myself today'

We end with Mrs Alexander's meditation on the cross, 'There is a green hill far away'. Here she sums up the traditional Christian view of the atonement in the words, 'He died that we might be forgiven, he died to make us good, that we might go at last to heaven, saved by his precious blood'. But perhaps closer to the heart of Victorian spirituality is the final verse: 'O dearly, dearly has he loved! And we must love him too, and trust in his redeeming blood, and try his works to do.'

'There is a green hill' (Bob Chilcott)

Outline: Sacred Moments

1   In 1926 the English pianist Myra Hess transcribed a lively Bach cantata into a more stately piano movement and the popularity of 'Jesu, joy of man's desiring' began. We tend to be rather shy of talking about desire because we fear that desire is a form of either envy, greed or lust. After Sigmund Freud many have come to suspect that desire for God is no more than sublimated sexual desire. But why not see things the other way round: all sexual desire is truly a sublimated desire for God. May you today meet the God who is the desire beyond all our desires.

'Jesu, joy of man's desiring' *(sung)*

2   Richard Gillard grew up in New Zealand and worked as a primary school teacher and in a warehouse. His life changed when he started writing his own songs in the late 1970s. In his most famous song, he describes what it means to walk alongside each other in discipleship and ministry. 'I will hold the Christ light for you in the night time of your fear', he says. 'I will share your joy and sorrow till we've seen this journey through.' It's a companionship that touches the most wondrous depths of shared human experience. May today be a day when you know solidarity with another so profoundly that in their struggle you discover the togetherness of God.

'Brother, sister, let me serve you' (*sung*)

5

Liturgy on the Edge

Introduction

What makes St Martin's unique is its breadth of relationships. It has regular contact with and occasional visits from members of the Royal Family, but its pews and environs are populated daily by those who sleep outside. It has a vibrant and dynamic congregation but perhaps a majority of those who come into the building do so for a concert or a meal or a shopping opportunity and may or may not get a sense of the liturgical life of the community. It hosts a range of special services, for the distinguished and noble and for the complex and vulnerable, many of which have outstanding choral music and carefully prepared liturgy and five or eight hundred well-wishers; but it also holds Morning and Evening Prayer each day for a half-dozen or dozen who themselves cover the full social and economic spectrum.

We close this book with insights and convictions about how to get the details of liturgy right – not so much in the advance production of orders of service or preparation of anthems or sermons, but in the manner, the understanding and the tenderness of recognizing what people are carrying in their hearts when they abide for an hour or a decade in the centre of a global city.

How to Welcome

Caroline Essex, Alison Lyon and Samuel Wells

Worship begins with an air of expectation. Welcome says, gently, warmly, 'Something wonderful is about to happen. It's the more wonderful because you've chosen to be a part of it. Thank you for making today a special day, just by being here.'

Welcome begins before any human encounter takes place – with prayerful anticipation of the surprises and epiphanies God is going to bring today. That makes any encounter with a newcomer or stranger like Simeon's delight in the appearance in the Temple of the 40-day-old Jesus – 'My eyes have (finally) seen your salvation!' Here is the long-expected one God has sent.

Most of this is done non-verbally, through body language: not giddy joy, but a warm smile, one that sparkles in the eyes and does not just exercise the lips. Most people respond well to being received with delight. Many take a lot of cues from the facial expressions of others, and can be quick to discern a human face that in repose can look unfriendly, even though the person might be listening intently.

The ministry of welcome is shared by clergy and laity. Greeters need to be genuine and kind; the service leader or priest who provides a focus for the welcome must communicate a desire to be right here, with these people, and nowhere else. We are about to begin liturgy, a work of the people – a joining together in worshipping God.

To speak of inclusive welcome means to be especially alert to how people coming from particular backgrounds or circumstances may find simply crossing the threshold of a church highly challenging. If for example you are a person who has experienced rejection of your identity in a church setting, it's a courageous step to risk coming into another church at all. In a different way, inclusive welcome needs to take account of practical obstacles to participation. Is the building wheelchair accessible? Is gluten-free bread and alcohol-free wine available for those who can't receive the elements in their conventional form? Is there provision made for sight-impaired people to follow the liturgy? Is it clear whether small children are welcome throughout the service, and, if not, what hospitality is offered to them?

Words carry the power to make or break relationships, and where a beautiful welcome can bring a congregation together, an unfortunate choice of words can result in people feeling excluded. Being genuinely inclusive means breaking down the barriers that the world commonly erects around us, so that whatever those who gather have brought with them, however unwelcome they might feel outside this space, they should experience the healing, reconciling love of God inside this space. Our responsibility is to transmit that scope of welcome to those gathered.

It is also a welcoming action to acknowledge if you have noticed that there are newcomers in the midst of the congregation. The welcome provides the opportunity to explain any special directions that might be required during the service. Sometimes these directions can be printed in service leaflets, but if this is not the practice it is worth finding a way to ensure that sufficient direction is given so that newcomers do not feel exposed by not knowing from one minute to the next what the 'regular' congregation might do.

Sometimes it will be necessary and appropriate to acknowledge significant events in the life of the church, or in the world at large, which have occurred during the course of a week, or since the congregation last met. The church must remain aware of, and touched by, events in the world. This frequently means acknowledging tragic incidents; but it can also be a chance to bring to mind joyful events too. On some occasions it might involve informing those gathered of the death of a well-known member of the congregation; the intercessions are not the place for this information to be shared for the first time.

The skill is to do all this briefly, warmly, but respectfully – recognizing that the newcomer has come to worship God, and the regulars' first duty is not to get in the way. Much can be done in a moment of silence, which reminds members of the congregation that they are gathered to tune in to the heartbeat of God. A brief, warm, inclusive welcome prepares us to encounter God in mystery, word and sacrament, and to be ready to be shaped by what God is doing and saying to us today.

How to Confess Sin

Caroline Essex, Alison Lyon, Samuel Wells

There's a paradox that Christianity is founded on forgiveness but many people come away from church because they fear God is angry and punishing while Christians are intolerant and judgemental. Confessing sin plays into our deepest insecurities and feelings of self-rejection. We're bound to be sensitive and to project anxieties on to others. Meanwhile a lot of things that aren't sin get tangled up with sin: failure, most commonly; lack of perfection, too frequently; shame, invariably.

For all these reasons the liberating and transformative moment of confession and absolution is best when it includes few, well-chosen words that presuppose prior honest reflection, articulate the longing for change, and avoid moralism.

Time-honoured, resonant words have an important place: 'We have followed too much the devices and desires of our own hearts ... we have left undone those things which we ought to have done, and we have done those things which we ought not to have done.' These are memorable, healthy, helpful. But there's also a place for succinct, crafted and new words, which perhaps engage more directly with themes of the day's service or of current events near or far. The ancient form of the 'Kyrie' – a threefold prayer to Father, Son and Holy Spirit – offers a regular but highly flexible shape. Four things are then needful: an introduction, a naming of wrong, a statement of contrition (which are together done threefold in a Kyrie), and words of absolution.

Inviting those gathered to confess together and shaping words of a Kyrie means encouraging each person to acknowledge several things: our equality before God (all have sinned); our genuine, willed seeking of what is unworthy (this was not a misunderstanding or misinterpretation); our need for God's forgiveness (we cannot repair the relationship on our own); and God's longing for us to come home to a welcome of joy and gladness.

Acknowledging our equality before God means recognizing our similarity to the tax collector who stood at a distance and beat his breast asking for God's forgiveness, rather than siding with the Pharisee who used his prayer to remind God how apparently faithful he had been. One of the tasks of confession is to unpeel the layers of self-justification we each wrap around ourselves, and to expose those areas of our life that we would rather not bring into the light. The prayers should be framed in such a way as to help each individual call to mind and admit the ways in which they have fallen short of the way of life to which God calls us. On other occasions it might be appropriate to use objects to symbolize the sins – such as pebbles, brought forward by each member of the congregation to represent the things they are sorry for, which are placed at the altar.

Recognizing our willed wrongdoing and realizing our need for God's forgiveness mean acknowledging that, through our sinful actions, we have broken the relationship God wants to forge with us, and that only God's grace can repair it. Through negligence, through weakness, through our own deliberate fault we get it wrong, we hurt our neighbour, we neglect to do something to help another in need, we focus on our own gain at the expense of others. But this is not simply a matter of individual conscience, between creature and Creator. Our actions have broken relationships with others, and by confessing together as the body of the Church, we are affirming our desire to restore that relationship with one another.

Appreciating God's longing for us to come home is the moment we open our eyes to grace: forgiveness is not earned – and it draws a line under what has gone before. It says that no matter what you've done or left undone, no matter how unlovable you think you are, God's love, which heals all, is poured out for you. For you. God wants to restore relationships with both the individual disciple and the body of the Church. God's overflowing grace is not contingent on anything we can do, save bringing to God a broken and contrite heart. This is a God who rushes out to welcome the prodigal, kisses him, puts rings on his fingers and kills the fatted calf: all part of the expression of sheer joy that the one who was lost has been found. This is the quality of the forgiveness and healing that is on offer to each one who turns back to God, and the confession should communicate something of that overflowing of grace and peace.

Once forgiveness has been sought, it must be given. This is really the most important thing a priest does: announce to a penitent sinner, or a congregation, that God has forgiven them. Short, uncomplicated: freedom, restoration, deliverance. And if all then stand to sing of thankfulness and joy, perhaps in the words of the Gloria, it's a conclusive statement that God has turned a burden on others into a carrier of others' burdens – for nothing is impossible with God.

How to Sing

Caroline Essex, Alison Lyon, Samuel Wells

As St Augustine said – or would have said, if he'd used gender-inclusive language – 'The one who sings, prays twice.' The fuller version, from his commentary on the Psalms says, 'He that singeth praise not only singeth, but also loveth him of whom he singeth. In praise, there is the speaking forth of one confessing; in singing, the affection of one loving.' Indeed, when we sing our feelings are more easily and more fully engaged, like a rugby fan at Cardiff Arms Park. The shared activity of singing together is an excellent way of unifying a disparate set of individuals into one group. As the best hymnwriters know, the combination of words and music, pattern and repetition, creates marvellous opportunities to join in.

Although church singing can sometimes smack of elitism (we have the better choir, we do/don't sing songs like the ones they do), at its best it is participative and collaborative – a way of being with one another that, as Augustine says, 'rouses our affection of whom we singeth'. Whatever our background and experience, we come together as we sing. We accommodate one

another – if the pitch is too high or too low, you can hear someone dropping or rising an octave so that they can continue; we
bear with those who habitually sing a half-beat in front of or
behind the rest of us.

To keep it rich we want not only to encourage participation,
but to facilitate it. To ensure singing is participative we need to
offer clear guidance about what is expected. In the service sheets,
it's simple to indicate which bits are for everyone to sing, and
which bits just for choir or cantor, or lower/upper voices. Hymn
tunes, especially new ones, can be included in service sheets, and
production times adjusted to make this possible.

To get the most out of singing requires good planning – so that
hymns fit the theme, are appropriate in content and style (perhaps quiet and reflective in Lent, exuberant for Easter Day and
Pentecost, anticipatory at Advent) and are presented in a way
that makes them straightforward to sing.

For 'standard' Sunday services at St Martin's these plans
are generated among the clergy and musicians. For occasional
services, others are involved as appropriate – for the St Luke
celebration, the service is compiled by the presiding clergy with
members of the Disability Advisory Group and the healing team.
The Bread for the World liturgy is created and led by different
groups in turn, who work with the pastoral assistant to create
the whole service including the hymns.

Choosing hymns that support a particular theme can offer a
chance to revisit old friends. When we celebrated our new pro-
cessional cross, we took the opportunity to include in the liturgy
'The old rugged cross'. There are few occasions when that would
be an appropriate choice, so we relished it when it came and
participated fully. Well-chosen hymns can be a wonderful way
of making the most of a particular theme or occasion, or adding
to the community's narrative of its own story. For those who can
offer commissions, they can be for hymns that the community
will sing together as well as for choir-only anthems.

Liturgy can be planned to suit our tradition and our habits,
and our resources. Across the 18 weekly services at St Martin's
there is scope for different shapes and styles. At the 10 a.m.
Eucharist each Sunday there are usually four or five participative

hymns and two choir anthems; our monthly evening healing service follows on from choir-sung Compline; at Great Sacred Music the hymns are carefully chosen to illustrate and amplify the theme of the week.

An offertory hymn might need to take four minutes on a busy Sunday; not all hymns can accommodate this. The elements are processed during the first verse and, to enable a suitable sense of climax as our gifts are offered at the altar, we include a flexible period of extempore organ between the penultimate and last verses. This then leads to a collective sense of completion as the final verse and the tidy procession of the offertory coincide.

Perhaps because it does engage our emotions and therefore our deep-seated beliefs of what is proper, feelings can run high about hymn-singing and the language it uses, especially among a diverse group of people with differing views. We explain our position on language with a statement in our service sheets (see footnotes) that seeks to account for occasional inconsistencies.

How to Intercede

Caroline Essex, Alison Lyon and Samuel Wells

To intercede on behalf of others is both an awesome privilege and a humbling responsibility. It is a privilege because the intercessor is trusted by the congregation to gather up the collective prayers of the people, and to articulate them in such a way as to facilitate that space for God and for us to communicate, either verbally or through groans too deep for words. It is a responsibility too, and appropriate preparation is necessary to ensure that we are communicating what is on the hearts of our community in the here and now.

There is room for many styles of intercession, but each should share some common characteristics. First, there should be no ambiguity in whom is being addressed: these are prayers addressed to God through the Son and inspired by the Spirit. Second, as the widow petitioning the judge and the Canaanite woman pleading for healing for her daughter illustrate, they are a place where our requests can be expressed boldly: 'bring peace', 'restore justice', 'heal wounds', 'pour out your love'. God is a God who forgives, heals, restores and sanctifies, and we are praying for God's power and grace to be extended to the situations for which we pray.

But while it can be appropriate to direct the prayers assertively, it can also be helpful to leave space for those gathered to bring the prayer they came to pray. This can be done silently: 'In a moment of quiet we lift before you, loving God, the people of one place that is on our hearts today, asking for your healing, justice and peace.' Or in smaller gatherings the congregants can be invited to contribute their own prayers, naming out loud situations or people close to them. In these cases the intercessor should highlight this aspect of the prayer before the prayers begin. Extemporizing in this way allows the congregation to feel the prompting of the Spirit and can add untold richness to the time of intercession, with the prayers being woven together from many diverse voices. Where such unstructured prayer is not used, responses can be helpful to break the prayers into themes and to enable the congregation to make the prayers their own; these can be printed in the service sheet and, if they are different from the norm, congregational comfort is increased by introducing and practising the call and response at the start of the intercessions. Typical areas for prayer are: the world/earth, the Church (local and universal), the local community, the sick of the parish, the dead and bereaved. A template such as this one offers a useful framework which can support succinct and well-organized prayers and can also enable the voice of the intercessor to emerge but not dominate.

In our highly connected, information-rich world, it can be tempting to feel that we need to pray for every situation. As the intercessor prepares, however, it can be helpful to dwell on the readings for the day, and read the sermon or talk (if it is available in advance to those preparing the liturgy), and the service sheet (where these are used). What are the common images and themes? Which of those themes resonate most strongly with my community, my region, my nation? Intercessions should not be confused with the notices – they are not a time for sharing information, nor are they the place for an extended explanation of world events or the opportunity to make a political point.

The organization of intercessions also requires thought. Being a place for lay members to make a contribution to the liturgy, it is important to ensure that there is a suitable diversity of contributors. Is the rota representative of the congregation? Are there assumptions you need to tackle as to who should be allowed to pray? Can you find novel ways of involving them? Involving children appropriately, asking them to craft prayers with an adult and pray them together, can be a beautiful way of involving young people in the mystery of worship, as well as being a blessing to the congregation in the simplicity and straightforwardness of what they request. Working in pairs models cooperation: voices from our Chinese-speaking and English-speaking congregations at Pentecost, or a British and a German voice on Remembrance Sunday. These ideas can come from the intercessors themselves, as well as the person compiling the rota. This person can also point out date-related themes when circulating the rota.

It is important that everyone can hear. Does your church use a microphone? Make sure it is on and working before it is needed. Is there someone interceding for the first time? Make sure they feel comfortable in what they will be asked to do, what cues to take, and how to pace what they pray. If you keep lists of names to be included, who updates these? How often? It can be helpful for the intercessors to meet together occasionally, say once or twice a year. They can share ideas and encouragement and be thanked for this important ministry that they offer.

How to Celebrate Gifts

Caroline Essex, Alison Lyon and Samuel Wells

The Eucharist is a model of a new society. Moved by the Scriptures, the people realize what they had thought were their own possessions, hurts, skills, experiences are in fact God's gifts, which will only find their true purpose in God's story. Accordingly the people bring forward the harvest of God's blessing – ordinary bread, celebratory wine – and the fruit of their labour – money, and at harvest perhaps food. More generally they may bring forward symbols of their community, tokens from the neighbourhood, and earnest prayers, perhaps those just offered by an intercessor.

In doing so they re-enact the feeding of the 5,000, where the loaves and fishes are the meagre offerings of the crowd, but become, when offered and transformed by God's story, abundant blessings beyond our needs or dreams. The whole drama inspires the congregation to locate every part of their lives within this larger story. Just as the Christmas story assembles rich and poor, male and female, heaven and earth to witness the intimate meeting in one body of God and humanity, so at the eucharistic table human endeavour and God's grace, labour and festivity, past sacrifice and future glory converge.

It's important that these vital dimensions of what's taking place are not missed. They can be highlighted by choosing particular words as an offertory prayer. They can become the focus of moments in the Church's year, like Harvest, Epiphany, Creation Sunday or Giving Sunday.

This is the most explicit place in the liturgy where the congregation gives thanks. The Great Thanksgiving is, in theory, about gratitude, but tends to focus on God's action in history. The Post-Communion Prayer is also about thankfulness, but tends to focus on the sacrament itself. Where does the congregation express joy that Nancy has got through her operation or that Ron has got home safe from his time in the military? Hannah prayed long to receive Samuel, and when Samuel was born she gave him straight back to God: the Offertory is the perfect place to make a visible gesture that all things belong to God, and we've been given the grace to cherish them for a period of time. In an informal setting, the person leading the service can simply say, 'Who wants to join the offertory procession and thank God today?'

In some contexts a 'mission of the month' can focus attention on how the church is spending its money beyond its own needs, and offer opportunities for sharing vision and communicating enthusiasm. Having an insight into such initiatives can enhance the thankfulness and community spirit of a church, enabling each to see that they are part of a wider whole in the church's life, contributing in some small way to work that they might not ever be in a position to do themselves.

This is also a significant moment to reflect on the diversity of gifts and their purposes. In the secular world gifts can express love and thanks, cement relationships and ingratiate the powerful or influential. In church, gifts are a fundamental statement that everything we have comes from God and that the first of what we have should therefore be returned in recognition.

But gifts aren't simply about individual thankfulness. They build community. The early apostles had all things in common and ensured there was sufficient for anyone who was in need. Jeremiah told the exiles in Babylon to 'Seek the welfare of the city where I have sent you into exile, and pray to the Lord on its behalf, for in its welfare you will find your welfare.' Giving our money to the church is part of our putting down roots, seeking the welfare of our city, town or village. This becomes a beautiful, deepening relationship: the more we put down our roots and invest our time and resources in the place where we are, the more we are nourished by the ground in which we find ourselves. In so doing, we make our thankfulness particular and we become one with the work of God in that place.

We are each God's gift to the world, and the celebration of the gifts we bring to the altar during the liturgy should recognize the wider meanings of the term 'gifts'. This is especially important in cultures where personal wealth is taken as a proxy for personal worth as a human being. We each bring other gifts that need to be acknowledged from time to time: our time, our energy, our talents. This can involve the presentation of something that the congregation has made together, or each member of the congregation can be encouraged to bring something that symbolizes for them the gift they feel they are to the wider church community, or the gift that they would like to be. When there is space in an act of worship to explore this more fully, such encounters can be very creative, enabling each person to bring into the liturgy something of themselves that perhaps is not often expressed or recognized in church.

How to Give Thanks

Caroline Essex, Alison Lyon and Samuel Wells

In the dawn prayers of the Jewish liturgy, each day starts by expressing thanks to God: *Modeh/Modah ani*. The notion of gratitude is indelibly woven into the individual and communal liturgical pattern. Anglicans are not blessed in this way, and so it is more challenging to build thankfulness into our liturgy.

It is a worthy challenge. Even though we have a General Thanksgiving, we seem to do very little of it. Some specific gratitude may be mentioned in some elements – in some hymns, or in the prayer after communion for example – and we might assume it to be implicit in the Gloria. We have regular slots to petition God (in the intercessions), to remind ourselves of God's story (in the readings and in the Eucharistic Prayer), to restate our beliefs (in the Creed). We might personally feel thankful for, and during, all those things. But our liturgies do not have places where we regularly make explicit our thankfulness. Does this gap affect our relationship with God, and our understanding of our relationship with God? What ways might be found to build thankfulness into our liturgy?

Ten lepers came forward for healing but only one went back to say thank you. Rather than assume that 10 per cent represents human nature, we hope to find more ways of fostering gratitude and of finding ways to build it into our liturgy (and so into our lives). At St Martin's we have tried a few ways to focus on gratitude and on its bigger sister, the sense that there is in fact enough to go around. We are fortunate in the assets that we have – our location, our history, our community – although we perhaps spend more energy feeling responsible for them than feeling thankful for them.

Thankfulness perhaps tends to be easier to express in the specific than in the general. Particular times of explicit gratitude include our patronal festival – for who could not be thankful for St Martin? Most patronal festivals will provide similar opportunities to celebrate what and who makes us what we are.

The farewells we say at funerals and memorial services also offer opportunities to celebrate our thankfulness for particular gifts and personalities. Did the departed know, however, of the thankfulness we are now expressing? In larger congregations it can be hard to find times to mark – and near impossible to keep track of – life events like new babies, new jobs, exam successes. Safer bets to thank individuals are occasions like annual meetings, retirements or handovers of church officers, at Easter to those who clean the church and dress it with flowers, at the conclusion of busy seasons like Advent and Christmas, with thanks to everyone who has contributed; a catch-all of those we might have forgotten is also helpful.

A few years ago our building renewal project gave us ample opportunities to express gratitude. As we left the building for a few months (to be St Martin's on Tour), we gave thanks for our people, the living stones, and together created an altar frontal that illustrated our gratitude for each of them and that, like singing, brought disparate individuals together into a visible whole. When we returned to the refurbished building we visited each of our new and refurbished spaces as part of the Easter Vigil, giving thanks for them.

Some times of ready thankfulness have been occasioned by things rather than by people: a new altar, new silverware. But we must not foster any myth that gratitude is for things rather than for our being. The challenge is to find ways to encourage and embed thankfulness, in liturgy and in life, from dawn and all through the day.

How to Give Notices

Caroline Essex, Alison Lyon, Samuel Wells

Besides music, notices are perhaps the most contentious part of a liturgy. The capacity to give offence is limitless. A vicar who ponders over every sentence of a sermon may approach notices as a moment of casual improvisation; but such is unwise, because what is included or excluded, the tone of voice or apparently dismissive air with which items are mentioned, and the sometimes unsuccessful but invariably revealing attempts at humour are often remembered long after the sermon is forgotten.

In an age of digital technology relatively few announcements are genuinely needed: there are accessible and widely used ways to convey information should people genuinely want to receive it. Notices of a practical nature are therefore primarily for the sake of newcomers, in how to access immediate participation (such as coffee after the service), or those too preoccupied to pay close attention to such information as is generally available (for example in a newsletter or weekly community email). The art of gently reminding a congregation of what is most pertinent, without insulting people's intelligence or commitment by assuming they can't or won't read what's written in front of them, is a complex one.

But notices aren't and never were primarily a practical matter. They are an opportunity to alter the tone of worship, to introduce humanity, humour, affirmation, and a topical tone. Some look for these in a sermon but the notices are the best place for them. For example, if a significant event has just happened or is about to happen nationally or locally, it can create a moment of intimacy and intensity if the person giving notices takes a moment for a brief, specific and heartfelt prayer. If a person is leaving the congregation to start a new adventure elsewhere, the notices provide a less formal setting to say some kind words, offer a gift or invoke a blessing. If a couple are about to get married, the person giving notices can encourage them and intercede for them.

More subtly, the notices can provide a balance if other parts of the service have seemed a little strident. If the sermon has taken a controversial stance, the notices can provide a softer, more engaging tone. If the intercessions have been full of woe, the notices can offer irony or humour. Particularly if the notices come shortly before the end of the service, this can be a juncture where one can mention big things coming up in the week ahead, in the life of the congregation, neighbourhood or nation.

But all this must be done briskly. Brevity is as crucial as warmth: this is not to become a focal moment in the liturgy. It must not become a commentary for insiders on matters many or most present know nothing about. It can, however, serve a dual purpose: if given during the clearing of the altar after communion it can shorten the service by a few minutes in a helpful way. Traditions will vary on whether to invite comments or additions from the congregation during the notices themselves – the skill of the person delivering notices is to ensure the liturgy keeps its shape and the sense of focus and devotion is not lost.

How to Send Out

Caroline Essex, Alison Lyon, Samuel Wells

What should technically be a highlight of the liturgy – for what could be better than to be sent out *to live and work to God's praise and glory?* – is at risk of being a bit of an anti-climax when most of us are only going as far as the coffee hall. It is not surprising that most people's minds are on their immediate next steps: a comfort stop, stacking hymnbooks, rota duties, coffee and welcoming visitors. For some people, the shaking hands at the door while leaving the building (or moving to a different bit of it) is a key part of the ritual, as well as an opportunity to share feedback or news with the clergy.

Planning for services is more likely to focus on those who are part of the recessional procession rather than those – the majority – who remain in church waiting for the organ voluntary to

finish. How do we create a sense of 'sending out' when the immediate practicalities seem to work against this?

For some liturgies it's appropriate to end with a communal
departure, a sense of going out together. At St Martin's we did
this at the start of the 2005–06 building renewal project when we
processed together from the church and, quite literally, locked
ourselves out. Pentecost also offers an opportunity to utilize the
drama of going forth together. But such opportunities are few,
and it can be challenging in more typical services to provide
appropriate focus on the sending out.

To ensure a clear climax to the service, with sufficient per-
sonnel, the notices can be given from the lectern after the
Post-Communion Prayer, which is given from the altar (and,
occasionally, while the altar is still being reverently cleared). The
notices themselves might often be of forthcoming activities that
will be in the 'sent out' portion of people's lives rather than the
church services part, and so support them in locating every part
of their lives in God's story.

Care may be taken that the notices, though clear and informative, are not the climax of the service and do not try to upstage it.
The focus then returns to worship, with an invitation to everyone
to stand for the blessing, also given from the altar. Then the final
hymn, during which clergy, choir, cross and chalice assistants
process towards the door. The wording of the dismissal often
invokes a sense of sending out, as with this Lenten version:

Walk with Christ on the way of the cross.
For it is the way of life and peace.
Thanks be to God.

As with all parts of worship, the sending-out works best when
the liturgy echoes and affirms the preaching and teaching, and
resonates with day-to-day activities. The call to inhabit the Kingdom, to live and work to God's praise and glory, is for seven
whole days, not one in seven; and this liturgical element is a
small but crucial prompt.